AUTHENTIC
ULTIMATE
EMPOWERING
BOXING
FITNESS
WORKOUT
TRAINING

Library and Archives Canada Cataloguing in Publication

Title: Ultimate boxing workout / Andy Dumas, Jamie Dumas.
Names: Dumas, Andy, author. | Dumas, Jamie, author.

Identifiers: Canadiana (print) 20190077263 | Canadiana (ebook) 20190077271 | ISBN 9781771613484 (softcover) | ISBN 9781771613491 (HTML) | ISBN 9781771613507 (PDF)

Subjects: LCSH: Boxing—Training. | LCSH: Physical fitness.
Classification: LCC GV1137.6 .D86 2019 | DDC 796.83—dc23

Published by Mosaic Press, Oakville, Ontario, Canada, 2019.

MOSAIC PRESS, Publishers
© Copyright Andy Dumas & Jamie Dumas 2019

Printed and bound in Canada.

Book layout and design by Andrea Tempesta

ONTARIO ARTS COUNCIL
CONSEIL DES ARTS DE L'ONTARIO
an Ontario government agency
un organisme du gouvernement de l'Ontario

We acknowledge the Ontario Arts Council
for their support of our publishing program

Funded by the Government of Canada
Financé par le gouvernement du Canada | Canada

MOSAIC PRESS
1252 Speers Road, Units 1 & 2
Oakville, Ontario L6L 5N9
phone: (905) 825-2130
info@mosaic-press.com
www.mosaic-press.com

AUTHENTIC ULTIMATE EMPOWERING BOXING FITNESS WORKOUT TRAINING

ANDY DUMAS & JAMIE DUMAS

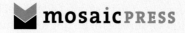
mosaicPRESS

www.ultimateboxingworkout.com

Acknowledgements
———

Our thanks go to Floyd Mayweather Jr., Mauricio Sulaiman, Victor Silva,
Tito Gonzalez of the World Boxing Council. Jill Diamond - WBC female championship committee;
World Boxing Champion Cecilia Braekhus. World Boxing Champion Alicia Ashley, Angie LaFontaine,
Tanya Caruana, David Hart, Antoinette Lowe, Anastasiya Kuznyetsova, Jun Ya Buki, Ryota Murata,
S.W.A.T. Health (Synergy Wellness Attitude Training) Port Credit.

Photographers
———

Nikola Novak, Kyla McCall, Naoki Fukuda, Lina Baker.

Photo Credits
———

Cover photographs by Nikola Novak
Instructional photographs by Kyla McCall & Nikola Novak *(www.nikpix.ca)*
Photo of Muhammad Ali by Jeff Julian
Boxing Champion photographs by Naoki Fukuda *(www.naopix.com)*
Additional photographs by Andy Dumas, Jamie Dumas

Disclaimer
———

Please note that the authors and the publisher of this book, and those others who have contributed to it, are not responsible in any manner whatsoever for any damage or injury of any kind that may result from practising, or applying, the principles, ideas, techniques and/or following the instructions/information described in this publication. Since the physical activities described in this book may be too strenuous in nature for some readers to engage in safely, it is essential that a doctor be consulted before participating.

Also by Andy Dumas and Jamie Dumas:
The One-Two Punch Boxing Workout, Old School Boxing Fitness,
Knockout Fitness, Successful Boxing and Fitness Boxing.

Boxing is the ideal workout for fitness and conditioning. Boxers are the best conditioned athletes in the world and *The Ultimate Boxing Workout* replicates the most beneficial elements of a boxer's practice to maximize results in the shortest amount of time.

People from around the world, both women and men, are discovering how to stay fit through boxing exercises. **Stamina**, **strength**, **speed**, **endurance**, and more are all within your reach through the *Ultimate Boxing Workout*.

Exhilarating interval workouts teach you the foundations of boxing training, body awareness, and proper execution of movements, resulting in a challenging and safe exercise program.

It is a fun, effective, and dynamic workout and includes routines that cover all aspects of boxing training.

Experience the challenging physical training of a boxer and get in the best physical condition of your life.

———

Chapters Include:

Ultimate Boxing Workout
Fitness Boxing Basics
Jump Rope Workouts
Punching Bag Workouts
Punch Mitt Workouts
Run Like A Boxer
Medicine Ball Strength Training
Active Muscle Stretches
Fuel Your Fitness
Boxing Interval Training Routines

Tap into a new way and approach to training. Learn how to box for physical fitness and discover the Champion within you! Connect with us on Instagram and Facebook.

Go to *www.ultimateboxingworkout.com* and check out your virtual gym.

Ultimate Boxing Workout Website
Your Virtual Gym

Experience the challenging physical training of a boxer and get in the best physical condition of your life. The Ultimate Boxing Workout website provides tips, demonstrations, and video support to start you on your journey to obtaining strong, taunt muscles, an enhanced cardiovascular system, and improved agility and coordination. Instructional videos of the boxing fundamentals, punches and combinations, shadowboxing, jumping rope, heavy bag training, and punch mitt drills are featured. This exhilarating interval workout teaches you the foundation of boxing training, body awareness, and proper execution of movements resulting in a challenging and safe exercise program.

The instructional videos on the website compliment the information presented in this book. Tap into new and exciting science-driven training systems and receive elite tips and exclusive videos from boxing and fitness experts. This exhilarating cross-training workout takes beginners and seasoned athletes to the next round of superb conditioning. Discover the Champion within you!

A new way and a new approach to training and learning how to box for physical fitness. Connect with us on Instagram and Facebook.

Go to *www.ultimateboxingworkout.com* and check out your virtual gym.

Contents

Andy Dumas

'KNOCK THE BOREDOM OUT OF YOUR WORKOUTS'

The Ultimate Boxing Workout is one of the most exhilarating cross-training routines ever developed. These dynamic training routines, distilled from boxing's unique fitness regimen, pack a punch like no other. This Ultimate Boxing Workout is derived from the motivating training techniques of the world champion boxers.

Dynamic intervals routines are the heart and soul of the Ultimate Boxing Workout. Energizing drills are incorporated for the jump rope, the heavy bag, punch mitts, the medicine ball, and roadwork training. Jump rope training results in faster foot speed, agility, and quickness. Hitting the heavy bag is a primal therapy of sorts and a tension release not found in any other workout. Each punch you throw on the heavy bag allows you to feel your own power. Fast and quick reaction time and responses are attained from training on the punch mitts. Your muscle development is enhanced by performing medicine ball drills and weight training

Jamie Dumas

"EMBRACE THE CHALLENGING PHYSICAL TRAINING OF A BOXER AND GET IN THE BEST PHYSICAL CONDITION OF YOUR LIFE."

exercises. Roadwork training generates an enhanced cardiovascular system and a greater aerobic capacity. The stretching exercises included in each workout will help you to maintain healthy and flexible muscles.

We have designed multiple workouts options for jump rope, heavy bag, punch mitts, and strength training with the medicine ball. These individual workouts will prepare you for the Boxing Interval Training System: The Basic Workout, The Contender's Workout, The Champs's Workout, The Twelve-Round Challenge and The Fifteen-Round Challenge. All workouts provide day-to-day progression and give you rewarding results. Start at a level that will challenge you, but one which will also fit into your current fitness level and lifestyle. Embrace the challenging physical training of a boxer and get in the best physical condition of your life.

Andy and Jamie Dumas

ANDY

Have you ever wondered why boxers, both men and women, are in such great physical condition? Have a close look at their strong, taut, conditioned muscles, their developed cardiovascular system, their superb agility and coordination. It is truly amazing! It is not accidental but as a result of boxing's unique training workout.

Fitness boxing has been discovered and is sweeping North America and spreading world-wide. Fitness Boxing offers something very unique. Unlike conventional workouts, boxing is not a means to an end, but is an end in itself. The punching bag exercises, for example, offer not only fitness and strength but also a very intense sport experience. The agility, coordination and

▼ Cliff Dumas Sr. after a fight (left)

spontaneous creativity required to exercise on the punching bag far exceeds the mental stimulation achieved with treadmills or stair climbing machines. And just knowing that you can pound the heavy bag for four or five rounds heightens your sense of security and personal confidence.

Balance, consistency, and discipline are needed to be successful in any fitness program but most importantly in fitness boxing. These values were passed on to me by my father, Clifford "Kippy" Dumas. His career as a professional boxer (in the 1940s and 1950s) took him all over the United States and Canada. Originally from Windsor Ontario, he fought in his hometown, as well as Detroit and Chicago. He was the sparring partner to middleweight champion Jake "The Raging Bull" LaMotta in preparation for the title fight with Sugar Ray Robinson. My father had the unusual distinction of being the first professional boxer of the modern era to win two bouts on the same night! After knocking out his scheduled opponent in the first round, he was invited back for an encore match, and won a decision. His life-long passion and commitment for staying healthy and physically fit still inspires me today.

In my early teens, I received my first heavy bag. My dad and I hooked up a chain around this great old tree in the back yard. He showed me how to wrap my hands, put on my boxing gloves and he said one word - go! Four rounds later, I was completely exhausted. I discovered that pounding the heavy bag is a great source of tension release, a genuine primal therapy. Not only does it burn serious calories and tone muscles, it also benefits the psyche. I was hooked from that moment on. This was the beginning of my passion for the "Sweet Science". To this day it's still the toughest workout I've ever done.

▲ Muhammad Ali

Exhilarating cross-training intervals routines are the heart and soul of the fitness boxing and our method in **Ultimate Boxing Workout**. Energizing drills are incorporated for jump rope, shadowboxing, the heavy bag, punch mitts, the medicine ball, roadwork training and stretching exercises.

Over the years I've been fortunate enough to spend time with some of the greatest boxers to ever lace up the gloves, legends such Alexis Arguello, Roberto Duran, George Foreman, Sugar Ray Leonard, Evander Holyfield, Marvelous Marvin Hagler, Thomas Hearns, Lennox Lewis, Ken Norton, and Floyd Mayweather Jr., to mention a few. I had the opportunity to meet and spend time with my idol Muhammad Ali on many occasions. For decades Ali has inspired millions around the world to be the best that they can be.

I hope this book motivates you to stay healthy and fit, and in some small way inspire you to be the best you can be.

JAMIE

To strive for one's personal best the mind, body, and soul must be nurtured and cultivated. Each intertwines with the other and with commitment, persistence, and the resolution to follow through on your dedication, each one of us will accomplish our goals of personal best.

As a young child, I had the opportunity to engage in the splendour and demands of dance classes, specifically ballet. The training involved hours and hours of rehearsal, developing strong, lean muscles, conditioning the heart, and refining movements to produce precise execution and ultimate physical conditioning.

Adele McGovern, my dance instructor, was one of the greatest inspirations in my life. Her career dates back before the opening of the New York's Radio City Music Hall, before the erection of Toronto's O'Keefe Centre, and before the establishment of the National Ballet School of Canada. As reported by Rita Daly, The Toronto Star, "She also taught tap dancing at a New York school a year before Hollywood's dance Maestro Gene Kelly did. In fact, he took over her class."

Throughout my childhood, adolescence, and into my adult life, I studied ballet with Miss Adele. Many happy moments and very rewarding hours were spent in her home studio. Ballet supported and gave me a great basis for my other physical endeavours and a healthy and fit lifestyle.

Andy introduced me to the world of boxing. The similarity between boxing and ballet are numerous and include athleticism, commitment, intensity, focus, and passion. Both demand thousands and thousands of hours of training, creating superior musculature, the execution of strong and perfectly timed movement, and finely tuned focused attention. This gives one a great sense of appreciation, empowerment, and extreme physical conditioning.

The Ultimate Boxing Workout takes you on journey toward getting in the best shape of your life. The easy to follow instructions and workouts will help you in achieving improved agility, speed, cardiovascular conditioning, core strength, muscle mass, and balance. This training will also assist in the loss of unhealthy fat, promote active healthy aging, and counteract disease and illness. The human body is meant to move and to be challenged in order to develop and improve.

Become your own personal best and make the commitment to *The Ultimate Boxing Workout*.

▼ Adele McGovern

11

MEN'S BOXING MADE ITS DEBUT AS A COMPETITIVE OLYMPIC SPORT IN ST LOUIS IN 1904. WOMEN'S BOXING HOWEVER, WAS LIMITED TO EXHIBITION BOUTS. IT WOULD BE DECADES BEFORE FEMALE BOXING MADE ITS OFFICIAL DEBUT IN THE OLYMPICS.

In the 1970s, female boxing was considered to be nothing more than an opening novelty act. The women of this era, however, trained hard, demonstrated high skill levels, and opened up the door for many of today's female boxers.

In 1988 a revival of female boxing took place when Swedish Boxing Association sanctioned female boxing matches. The British Amateur Boxing Association sanctioned its first boxing competition for women in 1997. USA Boxing Association eventually agreed to develop a national women's amateur division. There are well over 2,000 registered female boxers in the United States.

During the 1990s, women's professional boxing peaked in popularity with world champions like Bonnie Canino, Christy Martin, Laila Ali, Licia Rijker and Laura Serrano. The World Boxing Council (WBC) sanctioned women's world championship bouts and fights are now held in more than 100 countries worldwide. According to The Amateur Boxing Association of England, there are nearly 1000 registered female boxers in Britain, up from 70 in 2005.

Jill Diamond, of the WBC female championship committee says, "The WBC was the first of the recognized, non-gender belts given to women. It was a tremendous shot in the arm for woman's boxing. With the belt came recognition, better pay and finally, validation. Outside of the USA, woman's boxing really began to thrive. Within the USA, it was alive and punching, but in my opinion, the culture, and more importantly, the major promoters and TV networks, didn't give it the exposure it needed. And then came the economic crash a couple of years ago. I know from my own experience as head of the Female Championship Committee for the NABF (North American Boxing Federation), and co-chair for the WBC, woman's boxing took a hit. No one was taking chances even though we all know that when a good woman's fight appears on a card, people go wild.

"Women take the same risks, train as hard as the men and deserve the same respect. Things are looking better now, and my hope, like all people who are genuine fans, is that the Olympics will give women's boxing a needed boost. It has already garnered a lot of PR for the women involved, and it will be the first time women's boxing will be seen on national TV. It will bring more women into the gym and possibly encourage more marketing deals for the athletes. I think the future is bright."

The Olympic style of boxing is the basis of the sportsmanship of amateur boxing, and many of the great male professionals started in the world of amateur boxing and Olympic glory – men like Muhammad Ali, Joe Frazier, George Foreman, Evander Holyfield, Sugar Ray Leonard, Lennox Lewis, Floyd Mayweather Jr., and Oscar De La Hoya. Amateur boxing often gives the professional boxing arena its next outstanding contestants. It is a great training field to learn, practice, and develop into a professional boxer.

▼ Layla Ali

> "WOMEN TAKE THE SAME RISKS, TRAIN AS HARD AS THE MEN AND DESERVE THE SAME RESPECT. THINGS ARE LOOKING BETTER NOW, AND MY HOPE, LIKE ALL PEOPLE WHO ARE GENUINE FANS, IS THAT THE OLYMPICS WILL GIVE WOMAN'S BOXING A NEEDED BOOST"
>
> —Jill Diamond
> *WBC Female Championship Committee*

In 2009, International Olympic Committee (IOC) president Jacques Rogge announced the inclusion of women's boxing in the Games in London in the 2012 Olympics. British sports minister Gerry Sutcliffe remarked: "This move is a massive boost for women's boxing and will help raise the profile of women's boxing at all levels."

Great Britain's, Nicola Adams, became the first woman in history to receive an Olympic boxing medal, winning a gold medal at the 2012 Olympics. Nicola Adams achieved another milestone, winning gold in the flyweight boxing division in the Rio Olympics, 2016. Adams stated, "It feels absolutely amazing, especially to be able to think to myself that I've created history and I'm now the most accomplished British amateur boxer of all time." Certainly, female boxing will benefit from the positive worldwide exposure that the Olympics has provided.

Cecilia Braekhus, WBA, WBC, WBO Female Welterweight Champion, states, "With women boxers being able to compete in the Olympics for the first time in London, this exposure makes it easier to persuade promoters and television to put on female fights in the

United States. When I started to box, it was unheard of for girls to box where I came from. It was really tough in the beginning. But I'm so lucky, because I grew so much, and I got so strong and so tough out of that. I wouldn't change that for anything. Today, I can look with joy at the girls fighting in the Olympics and getting more attention and money from the sponsors and promoters, and it's just with big, great joy that I see this development that has happened over the last 10 years."

> **"AS A BOXER YOU ARE THE SUM OF ALL OF YOUR TRAINING. IT IS IN THE PROCESS OF LEARNING AND PERFECTING TECHNIQUE, DEVELOPING SELF-DISCIPLINE, SELF-CONFIDENCE AND INNER TOUGHNESS THAT WILL HELP YOU BECOME A SUCCESSFUL BOXER."**
>
> —Cecilia Braekhus
> *WBA, WBC, WBO Female Welterweight Champion*

The men and women who embrace the challenge of the sweet science are attracted to the thrill of the sport. "As a boxer you are the sum of all of your training. It is in the process of learning and perfecting technique, developing self-discipline, self-confidence and inner toughness that will help you become a successful boxer. It requires an inner desire and dedication to build the skill, agility, power, and conditioning to compete in this sport."

Female boxers are as committed to their craft as the male counterparts. These athletes are disciplined and dedicated to learning the sport and reaching the highest level of boxing ability and expertise.

UBW

The Ultimate Boxing Workout is derived from the ancient history of boxing. It is challenging with many rewards including the development of athleticism, sportsmanship, physical and mental conditioning, and self-worth. Work the fundamentals and develop the physical conditioning, endurance, agility, and style. Prepare as though you are training for the championship of the world.

Photo by: Lina Baker @seeyouringside

▼ Cecilia Braekhus, WBA, WBC, WBO Female Welterweight Champion

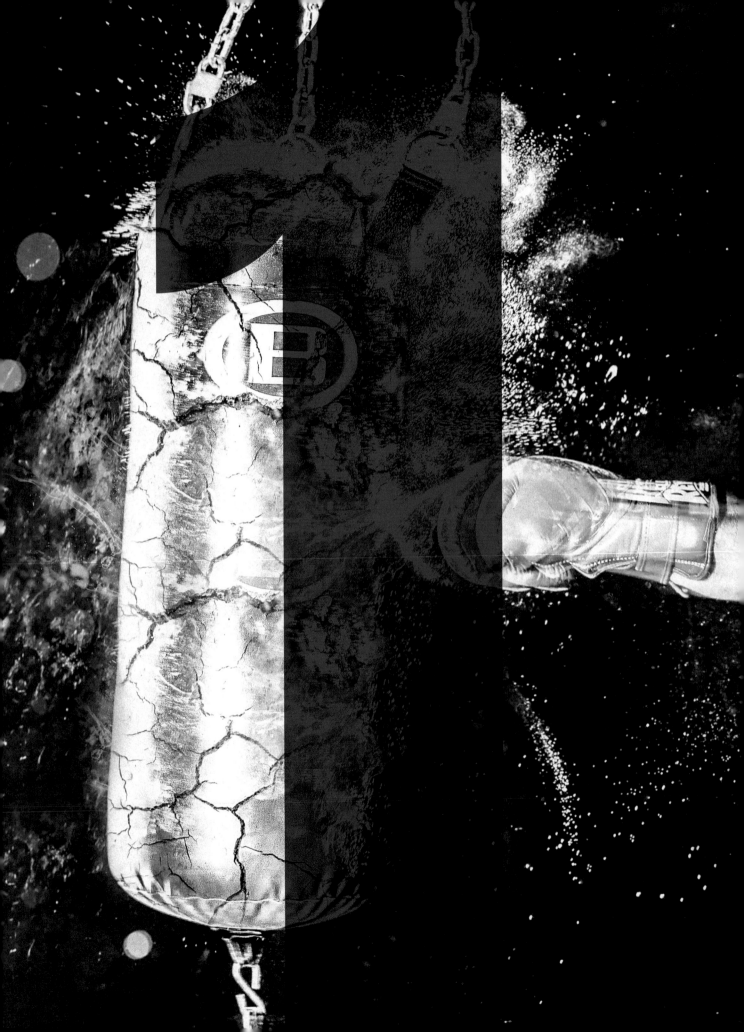

THE ULTIMATE BOXING WORKOUT

BOXING IS AN ANCIENT CRAFT THAT HAS EVOLVED FROM BARE KNUCKLE PUGILISM INTO THE LAS VEGAS SPECTACLE TO WHICH WE ARE NOW WITNESS. IT IS A DISCIPLINE WITH RULES, DECORUM, AND METHOD. AT THE HIGHEST LEVEL, BOXERS MUST BE IN SUPERB PHYSICAL CONDITION, AND EXHIBIT MENTAL COMMITMENT AND DRIVE.

For those who choose not to jump into the ring but rather follow the training techniques of the craft, they will find the skills that they gain will be easily transferable to other sports. A racquet sport player will find that the balance, agility, and strengthening associated with a boxing workout will only help their game. A baseball player likewise will find conditioning that will accentuate both their offensive and defensive strengths, as well as build on their hand/eye coordination. Cyclists, runners, hockey players, and soccer players will find that stamina increases from following the regimen of The Ultimate Boxing Workout. The Sweet Science compliments all sports. We encourage everyone, whatever game is their passion, to include The Ultimate Boxing Workout as part of their fitness training. You will never regret it! You will be accessing a sport that is completely versatile and creative.

Boxing will never cease to surprise you as you continue to learn its methods and philosophy. You will be better as an athlete and you will have fun!

Boxing Burns Serious Calories
The Ultimate Boxing Workout incorporates high-intensity training intervals and this causes a spike in the heart rate. The short rest period following the high intensity interval allows the heart rate to normalize. These short energy bursts are incredibly efficient in fat burning. You can expect to burn around 200 and 400 calories for an average 30-minute training session.

Boxing Knocks Out Stress
In addition to all the physical benefits, boxing has an emotional benefit. Why? Because it helps to alleviate stress. This is accomplished when hitting the punching bags or punch mitts, providing a primal therapy of

sorts. Boxing training can improve your mental state since you need to be alert at all times to focus on your technique and combinations. It is a great form of mental exercise.

These authentic boxing workouts have been developed over years, working with some of the world's best boxers and trainers. The Ultimate Boxing Workout is for those who want to experience the type of training a boxer goes through to get into top shape. This is the place where boxing and fitness meet in perfect balance. As you start your fitness boxing journey, this book will offer you the best of both worlds.

Benefits of Exercise
The physical and psychological benefits of exercising are numerous including weight control, the reduction of such diseases as cardiovascular disease, type 2 diabetes, and some cancers. Staying active and following an exercise program will increase bone density, as well as diminish joint pain. Muscle strength is improved and the aging process is slowed down. Exercising elevates self-esteem and has a positive effect on mental health.

VIEW FROM THE CHAMPS

Alicia Ashley made boxing history by claiming WBC female super bantamweight title, at the age of 48 making her boxing's oldest champion, male or female, surpassing Bernard Hopkins by 2 weeks. She is also holds the Guinness World Record as oldest champion.

"I CONSIDER BOXERS TO BE ONE OF THE BEST-CONDITIONED ATHLETES BECAUSE OF THE AEROBIC, ANAEROBIC, AND STAMINA INVOLVED. BOXING IS A FULL BODY WORKOUT."

—Alicia Ashley

Alicia Ashley

Cecilia Braekhus, WBA, WBC, WBO Female Welterweight Champion, states, "Our training is very special and it covers the entire body. You have to be 100 per cent fit otherwise you are in trouble. The conditioning is very popular in fitness studios. I know a lot of people who take boxing training just for fitness reasons. There is no better training for your overall fitness".

"I like the diversity and all the different elements of boxing training. The mental part, the strength, the technical part, the dancing, the footwork… and then, on fight day, it´s just you in the ring. The whole sport is really fascinating. You can learn something new every day. Hang in there and fight for your dream. You can do almost everything if you really want it and work hard."

PHYSICAL ATTRIBUTES OF SUCCESSFUL ATHLETES

The skills and physicality of athletes vary from sport to sport, however there are twelve general physical attributes all great athletes must strive to achieve. These twelve characteristics can all be improved by following the Ultimate Boxing Workout.

Cecilia Braekhus

1. Cardiovascular/respiratory endurance

The ability of the heart, lungs, and blood cells to gather, process, and deliver oxygen-rich blood to the working muscles tissues.

Boxers must have the endurance to perform at an optimal level for the entire length of the fight. Maintaining the same level of intensity from the first round to the last. This is achieved with skipping, heavy bag training, and punch mitt routines.

2. Stamina

The ability to sustain prolonged physical or mental effort.

Physical stamina levels can be significantly improved with the unique workout elements of boxing training. To achieve improved fitness levels stamina or endurance is a key component.

3. Strength

The ability of a muscular unit, or combination of muscular units, to apply force.

When in the ring, strong, powerful punches are essential for a boxer. By delivering forceful punches repeatedly on the heavy bag, overall strength is developed. The upper body, shoulders, arms, core, and leg muscles play an important role in producing strong punches.

4. Speed

The ability to minimize the time cycle of a repeated movement.

All great champions shared one great attribute: speed. Speed is needed to avoid getting hit by punches and to land punches. Throwing rapid-fire punches and reducing the amount of time between the strikes improves striking speed. Punch mitt training and speed bag training develop muscle memory and improve speed and reaction time.

5. Power

The ability of a muscular unit, or combination of muscular units to apply maximum force in minimum time.

Power is the combination of strength and speed. Boxers utilize both of these elements to be successful in the ring. To deliver punches with precise, explosive power, the muscles of the arms, upper body, core, and legs are trained. The heavy bag is the perfect piece of equipment to improve power.

6. Balance

The ability to control the placement of the body's centre of gravity in relation to its support base.

Boxers are always on the move and must have a sense of how to maintain a strong centre of balance. They need to be able to throw punches from awkward angles and be able to move to maintain their equilibrium after exchanging punches. Jump rope and punch mitt routines train and improve your balance and ease of quick movement.

7. Coordination

The ability to combine several distinct movement patterns into a singular distinct movement.

Boxers develop and execute synchronized punching combinations matched with defensive moves and balanced footwork. When working on punch mitts drills, your coordination is cultivated by throwing and executing synchronized punching combinations and matching this with balanced footwork. Also, speedbag training improves hand-eye coordination and timing.

8. Flexibility

The ability to maximize the range of motion at a given joint.

Boxers need to be agile to avoid incoming punches by slipping and ducking. Flexible muscles allow for quick movement changes and prevent the risk of muscle tears and injuries to the joint regions. To execute any sports related movement, your muscles need to be supple and reactive at the same time. An effective stretching routine is incorporated into the Ultimate Boxing Workout.

9. Agility

The ability to minimize transition time from one movement pattern to another.

Boxers train to be light on their feet, allowing for free-flowing transitions and a variety of punch sequences to be administered. Shadowboxing, jump rope, and foot work drills help to improve agility.

10. Accuracy

The ability to control movement in a given direction or at a given intensity.

Boxers train to develop the delivery of the perfect punch or punch sequences to the desired location. Working on the double-end bag, speed bag, and focus mitts all challenge and improve your accuracy.

11. Focus

Concentration on the task at hand. Focus on technique, being in the moment and doing your best.

In no other sport is it more important for an athlete to be 'in the moment'. Good boxers have to be one step ahead of their opponents for the entire bout. They must maintain perfect concentration for every second of every round. Punch Mitts, also known as Focus Mitts, is a great training routine to sharpen focus and concentration.

12. Commitment

Mental commitment and drive ensuring adherence to a training schedule and the goal at hand.

Boxing champions have the commitment and the intense mental focus required to succeed. Great boxers take pride in the process of developing a strong, lean, healthy body so their every move is executed with perfection. Boxing training encompasses every element required for total body fitness.

▼ Training Effect

If you want to achieve the physicality of a great athlete, the quick reflexes, agility, balance, power, and coordination, then you need to train like one. The Ultimate Boxing Workout mimics the training techniques of the best-conditioned athletes in the world. It offers variety and is both challenging and fun. One of the most difficult challenges when pursuing a healthier and a more active lifestyle is being consistent and sticking with the training. The key is to stay inspired and motivated with your workout to get the maximum benefit from your commitment.

TALE OF THE TAPE

Each one of us has distinct and unique abilities, capabilities, and capacities. Your current fitness level, as well as the rate and degree of improvements in your fitness status are directly influenced by your age, gender, heredity, past physical history, and your current fitness level. It is helpful to understand how your body develops and adapts to training.

In boxing the term, the 'Tale of the Tape', refers to an athlete's prefight stats. The information includes measurements, such as height, weight, reach, and age. From a fitness point of view this phrase has equally important implications. Everyone has his or her own unique body type, musculature, fast or slow twitch muscle fibres, cardiovascular fitness, a base starting fitness level, percentage of fat, and responsive adaptation rates.

The Training Effect

Fitness training places physical demands on your body resulting in improvements in the capability, functionality, and capacity when exercising.

Your level of physical fitness is indicative of your level of commitment to training and when the appropriate physical demands are introduced into your training program, your fitness level improves. However, when the exercise demands are not sufficient or cease, your fitness level plateaus or may decline. When a fitness plateau is realized it is time to alter your workout program change the stresses on the body and introduce new, different, and additional demands.

A training effect results when the body's musculature, cardiovascular, and respiratory systems adapt to the demands of the physical effort. A threshold demand is necessary for improvements to occur. If the demand is not sufficient, then changes will not occur. If the demand is too great, then injury or over-training can occur.

> "PERHAPS THE GREATEST BENEFIT OF AN ENTERTAINING WORKOUT IS THE MOTIVATION TO EXERCISE WHEN YOU OTHERWISE MIGHT NOT TRAIN."
>
> —Floyd Mayweather Jr.

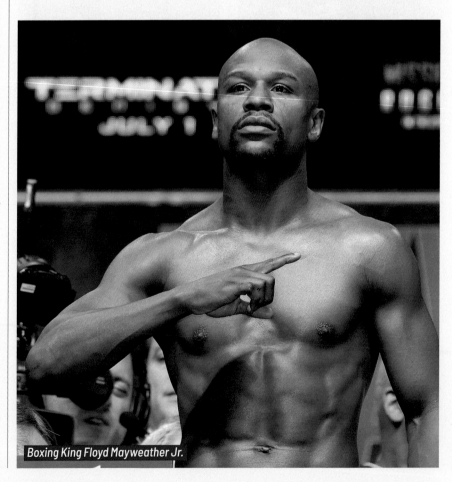

Boxing King Floyd Mayweather Jr.

The heart, lungs, muscles, joints, and the immune system all adapt to exercise. The muscles get stronger, the joints become sufficiently lubricated, the bones become stronger and thicker, the heart pumps out a greater volume of blood to the working muscles and the lungs provide a greater percentage of oxygen to the circulatory system.

Factors involved in this adaptation process include overload, specificity, reversibility, as well as individual differences. All of these will determine the rate and type of physical gains you will obtain.

Overload Principle

The stress or demands of a movement or activity must be greater than what the body is accustomed to, in order for an overload to take place. When additional exertion is required to execute a movement, increased demands are placed on the varying systems of the body. Just by starting a different training program, new demands or overloads are placed on the body and fitness level improvements can be acknowledged quickly.

When your body adapts to the training overload placed upon it, accommodation will occur. Accommodation is when there is no longer any additional progress in your fitness level. It is the result of the body successfully adapting to the training stimuli and is often referred to as reaching a plateau.

As previously mentioned, a fitness level plateau is reached when limited or no improvements in your fitness level is seen. To achieve improvements a new overload must be added to your training program. To avoid or overcome a fitness level plateau and to progressively improve your physicality it is important to provide sufficient variety in your training regimen. Ways to provide variety in your training are to reduce or alter the rest time between the exercises, change the speed or the rate at which the exercise is executed, change the number of sets and/or repetitions of an exercise, change the exercise or the order in which you perform the exercise, and increase the load or demand. The key is to provide variety and various ongoing overloads to the body. Boxing training is versatile and offers dynamic and countless training options.

Exercise choices and time allotments need to be considered, and rest intervals are very important to maximize the overload tensions. With adequate rest and sufficient recovery time, the body will get stronger and fitness levels will improve. If you are new to fitness training, it will take the body a few months to adapt to the new demands of the activity and variety is not as imperative.

▼ Specificity

Specificity

The body adapts specifically to the type of stress and demands that are placed upon it and therefore the type of adaptation results from the actual training regimen. A good training program places stress on the muscles that are required to perform a specific movement and also include muscle movements that are as close as possible to the activity that you want to improve.

There are a number of types of specificity such as: speed of a muscle contraction, the sequence of a movement, the speed of a movement, specific motor patterns and synchronicity, and the power behind the movement. Boxing training offers an exhilarating variety of exercises and workout overload options for continued athletic progress, giving an effective and invigorating total body workout.

Deconditioning Syndrome

If you do not exercise and do not place specific demands or an overload on the body, your fitness level not only plateaus it will reverse to a lower level. When a muscle is not used or has been immobilized, atrophy will occur. This means the strength and the mass of the muscle will decrease. Your joints lose lubrication, your bones become brittle, your heart rate increases, and less oxygen is delivered to the working muscles. You become deconditioned.

TRAINING INTENSITY

Train with passion, commitment, and consistency to achieve the greatest return from your workout. There will be workouts when your body will respond efficiently and there will be workouts when you may feel sluggish and uninspired.

Rate of Perceived Exertion (RPE)

How hard do you have to work to achieve the fitness level you want? A simple method to measure and monitor how hard you are working or your 'exercising intensity' is to use a Rate of Perceived Exertion Scale: 0-10.

This scale is based on a 0-10 level chart rating how you feel when physically exerting yourself. While you are sitting in a chair at rest the exertion rating is zero. When you move your arms while sitting in a chair the rating is 1. Warming up before exercising helps to increase the blood flow to your muscles and the rating is 2-3. Walking at a moderate pace is a rating of 3. When it is very difficult to continue the activity for more than a minute, like sprints or speed work, the rating is 9-10.

RPE Scale

0-1 No exertion. Sitting in a chair and relaxed.

2-3 Light exertion. Your muscles are starting to warm up. Warm-up exercises, stretching, cooling down.

4-5 Medium exertion. Heart rate increases slightly, breathing slightly faster, and your body is getting warmer.

6-7 Moderate exertion. Your breathing increases and you will start for to sweat. Talking will become more difficult.

8-9 Hard exertion. Your breathing becomes more laboured and it is difficult to talk.

10 Hardest exertion. It is difficult to keep this pace for more than 1 minute then this is your limit. You will be unable to speak.

Regardless of your current fitness level or the type of training you are performing, using RPE to gauge your exercise intensity is effective and helpful. Basically, your effort, fatigue, or discomfort experienced during either cardio activities or resistance training can be correlated to the RPE Scale. The scale typically shows a linear relationship of how hard your heart is working and the quantity of oxygen being consumed with the amount of exertion you believe you are generating.

It is simple and uncomplicated, no equipment is required, and you do not have to stop the activity to get a reading. It is easy to continually monitor how you feel and therefore how hard you are working whether you are running, jumping rope, hitting the bag, or performing focus mitt drills. Adjust your workout intensity level up or down to correspond to the scale and then train at this desired rate. Learn to listen to your body and how you are feeling.

Knock the Boredom Out of Your Workouts!

The Ultimate Boxing Workout provides an exhilarating and fun alternative to help you achieve maximum results in the most efficient way possible. By choosing a workout with a wide variety of fitness training options, setting realistic goals for yourself, making physical activity a priority in your everyday life, and adopting a healthy diet, you can acquire a superior overall physical conditioning and well-being. Improvements in muscular strength and endurance, cardiovascular and respiratory endurance, flexibility, and body composition can be achieved with The Ultimate Boxing Workout.

▼ Knock the boredom out

FITNESS BOXING FUNDAMENTALS

PROPERLY MASTERING THE FUNDAMENTALS IS VITAL TO SUCCESS IN ANY ACTIVITY, GAME OR SPORT, AND THERE IS NO EXCEPTION IN BOXING TRAINING.

To develop and master the boxing fundamentals, consistently train with focus and purpose. This will create a stable base for you to build upon, allowing for your fitness level and skills to progress naturally. When developing new skills aim to make them a habit. A habit is a conditioned reflex that is the result of repetitive movements. The goal is to practice the fundamental skills until they become 'good' habits.

"I love the technical part of training, that to me is the most fascinating", says Cecilia Braekhus, Female World Welterweight Champion. "It's a combination of so many things. How you coordinate your footwork with your defence and offense, or the combination of balance and strength. That is really fascinating to me. You always keep learning, you are never done!"

THE TRADITIONAL BOXING STANCE

All moves in boxing originate from a balanced boxing stance. It is the foundation of smooth, steady movement that facilitates the delivery of effective punch combinations. It is essential that you develop a boxing stance that provides stability and allows you to move easily.

Finding the Right Boxing Stance for You

If your dominant hand is your right hand, adopt a 'traditional' or 'orthodox' stance. The left shoulder and the left foot are forward, allowing for the easy execution of the left jab. Developing a solid, left jab will allow you to set

up power punches such as the straight right. If your dominant hand is your left hand, then the right shoulder and right foot are forward, and you will utilize a right jab. This is referred to as 'southpaw stance'.

Throughout this book, all moves and combinations will be described from the classic/orthodox stance.

Feet and Legs

Proper foot placement is one of the most important elements for an effective boxing stance.

If your foot placement is incorrect, your movement will be ineffective and inefficient when shadowboxing, working the heavy bags, or working on the punch mitts. Your lead (front) foot should point toward your imaginary opponent. (The heavy bag and your

Foot placement

partner on the punch mitts are considered your 'opponent'.)

It is essential to start with a solid base to execute all moves. Stand with your feet shoulder width apart or slightly wider. Step backward with your right foot. The back or rear foot is behind and slightly off to the side of your lead foot and is never directly behind your front lead foot. This is the starting foot position for an orthodox, (right-hand dominant), boxer. Equally distribute your body weight between the lead and rear feet. If too much weight is placed on your lead foot it makes it difficult to move and step away quickly after you have thrown a punch. It also reduces the ability to pivot on the rear foot and decreases the power behind your straight right. Centre your body weight through the balls of your feet, with the heel of the rear foot slightly raised. The raised back heal allows you to move and respond quickly. Your lower body position should feel balanced and allow for easy movement in all directions. Keep your knees slightly bent allowing for better mobility, power, and a balanced movement. Make sure not to bend your knees too much, as this will result in clumsy and sluggish movement.

The Body

Your body position is angled and slightly sideways providing the smallest target area possible. Your front

Traditional boxing stance

shoulder, front hip, and forward foot line up. Keep your abdominals firm, and your shoulders slightly rounded, forward, and relaxed. Focus on the centre of your body and start all your movements from deep within your core. The power of your punch is generated from a strong, centred core.

The Arms and Shoulders

Hold your arms close to the sides of the body by the rib cage, with your shoulders relaxed and slightly rounded. The elbows are bent and pointing down and in, thereby protecting your rib cage and solar plexus. Keep both hands up by your face. Boxers are constantly adjusting the position of their arms in order to defend against head shots and body shots from their opponents.

The Hands and Fists

On Guard Position:
Keep your fists up high. This is the best position to deliver your punches. Close your fingers together to make a loose fist, with your thumb folding to the outside of the fingers and do not clench your fist too tight. Turn your fists inward slightly and keep your wrists straight and strong. The orthodox boxer often holds the right fist slightly higher, very close to the chin, and the left fist held just above the top of the left shoulder. It is from this position that all punches are executed. (Reverse for southpaws.) Your fists are always in the 'on guard position' unless you are throwing a punch.

The Head

Keep your eyes in the direction of the target, (the various punching bags or punch mitts). Your chin stays tucked in toward your chest and your head slightly forward and down. Once again, these movements are replicating the strategies of a boxer. This is the head space you need to be in when performing your boxing workout, (shadowboxing, hitting the bag, and striking the punch mitts).

KEYS TO SUCCESS

Keep your legs and feet in a balanced stance ready to move.

—

Point your front/lead foot in the direction of your target.

—

Point the toe of the back foot out slightly toward the side.

Ensure your body weight is equally centred through the balls of your feet.

—

Your rear foot is shoulder-width (or more) behind and slightly out to the side of your lead foot, and not directly behind your lead foot.

—

Your abdominal core muscles are contracted and held firm.

—

Keep your neck and shoulder muscles relaxed allowing for easier execution of the punches.

—

Stay on the balls of your feet with slightly bent knees. This allows for quick and efficient movement from one position to the next.

—

Your front shoulder, hip, and foot are aligned and your body angles toward the target.

—

Your arms are held close to the sides of the body with your elbows positioned by the rib cage.

—

Close your fingers in a loose fist, with your thumb resting over top of the fingers.

—

Your fists turn in slightly and are held high in the 'on guard' position.

▼ How to Throw a Punch

Focus on proper execution of your punches

How to Throw a Punch

It is important to develop a multitude of smooth and technically correct single punches before working on punch combinations. Proper execution of each single punch must be duplicated over and over in order to improve your skills. Practice with purpose and stay focused on throwing one effective punch at a time. Your muscles need to be trained to react quickly and simultaneously in order to produce effective punches. The basic punches that need to be mastered are the jab, straight right, hooks, and uppercuts.

The Left Jab

A fast, effective jab is a boxer's number one weapon. It sets up more powerful punches such as hooks and uppercuts. Throw the jab with speed, and accuracy. During any given round, whether shadowboxing or on the heavy bag, a multitude of jabs should be thrown continually.

In a boxing match the jab is the most frequently thrown punch in your arsenal, (about 65 to 70 per cent of the total punches thrown) and can be utilized as both an offensive and defensive weapon.

Stand in the classic or orthodox boxing stance, with your palm of your left fist facing you. Your hand in a relaxed fist. Your left arm snaps away from your body in a straight line toward the target. As your arm extends forward, your fist rotates and your palm faces down at point of impact.

▼ Left Jab

Fully extend your arm without any hyperextension at your elbow joint. Your shoulder follows through to protect your chin. When you launch the jab do not rotate your fist too early. Allow the rotation to flow from the movement that starts from your shoulder, extends through your elbow and then to your fist. Avoid the 'chicken wing' effect. This is when your elbow leaves the side of the body creating a sloppy and ineffective punch. This makes the punch powerless and ineffective.

After striking your target, bring your left arm back to the on-guard position quickly and along the same path of the delivery. Protect your ribs by keeping your elbows close to the sides of your body. Remember to keep your right hand by your face when throwing the left jab.

Throw jabs to a virtual opponent's head or body. When throwing punches to the body, bend your knees thereby lowering the position of your punch. This is far more effective than dropping your hands. Practice this when shadowboxing or training on the heavy bag.

Once the effectiveness and the timing of your punch improves increase your punch power by moving forward slightly as you launch your jab. To accomplish this, push off the ball of your back foot slightly and slide your front foot forward at the same time as you throw the punch. Your foot movement must be synchronized with your punch. Always execute your jab from a well-balanced position and breathe naturally exhaling as you launch your punch. Get in the habit of throwing fast, quick jabs. This is also referred to as 'snapping your punches'. To deliver a snapping punch, throw quickly having minimal contact time with the target and then return straightaway to the on-guard position.

The main purpose of the jab is to keep your opponent at a safe distance, distracted, and off-guard. Get in the habit of throwing crisp jabs at different angles while moving around the target.

KEYS TO SUCCESS

Elbow moves straight forward as you execute your jab. Do not lift it out sideways.

—

Winding–up or pulling back the fist is another common mistake. Practice in front of a mirror to ensure your jab is thrown straight out and returning straight back to the on–guard position.

—

Rotate your fist during the last third of the punch so your palm is facing down on impact. Focus on fully extending your arm and rotating your fist.

—

Throw plenty of fast, snappy, crisp jabs.

The Straight Right

The straight right, also referred to as the right-cross, is a power punch executed from the orthodox boxing stance. The straight right takes more time and more energy to execute than the jab.

Starting in the on-guard stance, your right hand is thrown from the chin as your rear shoulder thrusts forward. The fist travels in a straight line toward the target and rotates during the last third of the punch with your palm facing down. Power is generated off of your trail foot and the punch travels straight forward to the target.

Keep your core muscles tight to maintain correct alignment and a strong centre of balance. Remain on the balls of your feet with your right hip rotating forward as you launch your straight right. This simultaneous rotation of the right hip and right shoulder along with the push off of the ball of your rear foot, combine to produce a powerful straight right.

Keep your lead hand in front of the face ready to throw a follow up punch. As with the jab, ensure that you do not pull the arm or lift your rear elbow before throwing the punch. Finish the punch with your hips square to the target, your chin down, and both eyes on the target. Swiftly return to the on-guard position as you prepare to throw your next punch. More muscles are engaged and more energy is required when throwing straight rights.

▼ Straight right

KEYS TO SUCCESS

The punch is a synchronized body movement, with your knees slightly bent for easy rotation of your torso, shoulders and hip regions.

—

Make sure your shoulders and hips move together and your body weight is transferring from your back foot to your front foot when the punch is launched.

—

Execute the punch in a straight line to the target. Do not lift your rear elbow.

—

Stay up on the ball of your rear foot as you launch the punch.

—

The lead (jab) fist remains in the on–guard position. Do not let it drop as you execute the straight right.

FINISH THE PUNCH WITH YOUR HIPS SQUARE TO THE TARGET, YOUR CHIN DOWN, AND BOTH EYES ON THE TARGET.

Hooks

The hook is a short-range, semi-circular punch most often thrown with your lead hand.

The strength and velocity of this punch comes from the synchronization of the body pivoting while rotating through the hips and pressing through the feet. In order for hooks to be effective, they must be thrown at close range. It is not a wild punch, but rather a punch thrown with precision and control.

The Left Hook

With your hands in the on-guard position and your core muscles held tight, keep your knees slightly bent and your body weight centred through both of your legs. As you launch the punch, your left elbow lifts away from the rib cage and the underside of your arm is parallel to the floor. The elbow is kept at a 90 degrees angle throughout the delivery. Your shoulders and hips rotate clockwise and your lead foot pivots inward on the ball of your foot. Your wrist remains strong and your thumb points up allowing your knuckles to make solid contact. Quickly return your left elbow to the side of the body and your left fist up to protect the chin.

One advantage of an effective left hook is the short distance it travels to reach the target.

The left hook moves about one-third of the distance of the straight right, making it a very deceptive punch. The hook can be delivered to the body or the head. By bending your knees and lowering your body puts you in the ideal position to land hooks to the body.

The Right Hook

For an orthodox boxer, the right hook comes from your dominant rear hand. Pivot on the ball of your rear foot, quickly rotating your right arm, shoulder, body, and hips in one movement in a counter-clockwise direction. The right hook has a greater distance to travel to make contact. Your body moves the same way as when you throw a straight right but your right arm swings in a tight circular motion. You must step in closer to your target, as your arm is not extended fully. After the punch is thrown, quickly return to the on-guard position, fists up by your chin and elbows protecting your body.

The right hook is not utilized as much as the left hook in a boxing match since the opponent can easily detect the wide-hooking motion coming off of the back foot. When working the heavy bag, a flurry of short left and right hooks to the body can be thrown at close range .

▼ Left Hook

Uppercut

Uppercuts are powerful, close-range punches and can be thrown by either the left or the right hand. The punch travels in an upward arc motion toward the target. Like the hook, this punch is considered an inside punch and you must be close to the target. Uppercuts can be delivered to your opponent's body or the chin.

Right Uppercut

To launch the right uppercut, start in the orthodox stance, (left foot forward, right foot back), keeping your rear knee relaxed with a slight bend. Your right shoulder lowers to the right side of the body and the left fist stays high by your chin and head for protection. From this semi-crouching position, rotate your hips forward, throwing your fist upward in a rising arc toward the target. Your arm remains bent at the elbow, your wrist stays strong, and your right shoulder follows through with the rotating hips. Upon impact, square your hips

▼ Right Uppercut

▼ Left Uppercut

KEYS TO SUCCESS

Do not wind up or pull your arm back before throwing an uppercut.

—

At the time of delivery and follow through, your elbow remains bent at a ninety-degree angle for the most impact.

—

Use the power and strength behind your body by transferring your weight forward and in the direction of your punch.

—

Drive off the balls of your feet in order to execute the uppercut.

—

Do not lean backward onto your heel.

—

Keep your balance centred, with your core muscle held tight.

There are dozens of different ways to throw each punch depending on your body position, the timing of the punch execution, your body build, and individual idiosyncrasies. You can develop your own unique style of punching.

LEARN TO SET UP YOUR UPPERCUTS WITH STRAIGHT PUNCHES, BY MOVING IN CLOSE TO YOUR TARGET AND LAUNCHING THEM AT CLOSE RANGE.

front and keep your elbows bent at a right angle. All of this occurs simultaneously in one smooth movement. Return to the on-guard position as quickly as possible, ready for the next move.

Left Uppercut
The left uppercut is thrown by positioning your body in a semi-crouching position to the left side, with your left shoulder lowered and your body weight transferring to the ball of your left foot upon delivery of the punch. Keep the

punch motion tight, using an upward driving force from your hips and legs to increase the power of the punch on impact. An uppercut thrown from a long range will lose some of its power because the arm is no longer sufficiently bent at the elbow and the total body's force will not be transferred in the upward movement. Learn to set up your uppercuts with straight punches (left jabs and straight rights), by moving in close to your target and launching them at close range.

FOOTWORK AND MOVEMENT

High quality footwork is important in many sports such as soccer and tennis, but in no other sport is it more important than in boxing. Skilful footwork can get a boxer out of dangerous situations and provide counterpunching opportunities. Developing smooth and balanced footwork is also essential for an effective Fitness Boxing workout. Footwork should be calculated and have a purpose. Use your legs and feet to get you into and out of punching range. Stay relaxed and in control. Maintain your balance and stay on the balls of your feet. This will allow you to move smoothly across the floor.

Boxers such as Muhammad Ali and Floyd Mayweather Jr. took imaginative footwork and ingenious movement in the ring to a balletic art form. Watch footage of how their balance, rhythm, and ability to change direction looked almost effortless.

Forward Movement

Smooth footwork and balanced movement allow you to get into range to land your punches. Starting from the balanced boxing stance, push off the ball of your back foot as you move your front foot forward. Think in terms of 'pushing off' instead of 'stepping'. Both feet move almost simultaneously with your lead foot moving a split second first. If you take a large step with the front foot first, your weight will be placed on the heel instead of the ball of the front foot making it difficult to change directions quickly. Pushing off keeps you on the balls of your feet and allows you to move quickly and pivot easily.

Backward Movement

Boxers require quick, balanced movement to avoid an opponent's punches. Move backward by pushing off your front foot at the same time as the rear foot moves back. The purpose of this movement is to reset and plan your next move, either by throwing punches or moving once again in another direction.

Moving Left

Effortless lateral movement is essential for boxers.

Keep your feet shoulder-width apart in order to maintain your balance. To move left, push off your right foot as your left foot moves to the left. Stay in your boxing stance, (slightly sideways), and not standing square to the target. This movement is not a lunge and should be kept compact.

Moving Right

When moving to the right, push off your left foot as you move your right foot to the right. Always stay in the orthodox boxing stance when moving.

KEYS TO SUCCESS

When moving forward, push off the ball of your back foot at the same time as you move your front foot forward.

—

When moving backward, push off your front foot as your back foot moves backward.

When moving to the left, push off your right foot as your left foot moves to the left.

—

When moving to the right, push off your left foot as you move your right foot to the right.

—

Do not try to cover ground too quickly by lunging or taking huge steps. This will put you off balance and in an awkward position.

—

Do not cross your feet to change direction.

—

Come back to the balanced on-guard position quickly, keeping your front foot and shoulder in the direction of the target.

Boxer's Bounce

Boxer's bounce, also called boxing rhythm, refers to a style of boxing movement that involves energetic bouncing and footwork similar to jumping rope. It is generally a forward and backward movement that is

Bouncing rhythm

balanced and subtle. The punches are timed with the bounce motion. This style of footwork keeps you light on your feet, provides cardio conditioning, and burns more calories.

Watch old fight footage of all-time great fighters such as, Muhammad Ali, Sugar Ray Leonard, or Manny Pacquiao. Notice how their rhythmic bouncing styles of constantly moving forward, backward, and side-to-side would confuse their opponents and create openings to land their own punches. Their foot movement was smooth and perfectly timed with the release of their punches. Rhythmic footwork and constant movement, whether on the heavy bag, punch mitts, or jump rope will create a challenging workout and improve overall conditioning.

Executing the Boxer's Bounce

Start in your balanced boxing stance with your knees relaxed. Push off the balls of your feet, similar to jumping rope, and spring slightly forward, backward, and side-to-side. Stay on the balls of your feet while moving. Your heels do not touch the ground. To move forward push off the ball of your rear foot and land on the ball of your lead foot. To move backward, push off the ball of your rear foot and land on the ball of your lead foot. This light and 'springy' motion is very subtle with your feet lifting just a few centimetres off the ground. You must briefly stop the bouncing motion in order to set your feet and throw your punches before returning to the bouncing rhythm. Bounce then set your feet, punch, and repeat.

Each foot pattern should be calculated to put you in position to strike your opponent or avoid counter-punches from your opponent. Practice this style of moving in 20 or 30-second spurts while shadowboxing or hitting the heavy bag. Focus on moving smoothly in all directions while staying balanced.

SHADOWBOXING

Shadowboxing is simply the raw exercise of moving your hands, feet, and body like a boxer. Shadowboxing allows you to master the fluidity of a boxer's movement. The punches, footwork, and defensive moves are combined to create an exciting and rewarding fitness session and is performed without the need of a partner or a bag. The practicing of repetitive actions, allows you to commit the boxing movements to muscle memory. It is important to review the punching fundamental and ensure your execution is accurate.

Shadowbox at the beginning of your training session. It is a great way to warm up the muscles of the body and also prepares you mentally for the workout to follow. When shadowboxing always work on the correct execution of the punches and combined with foot movements. Often boxers will fill up their spare time between rounds of bag work and skipping with short bursts of shadowboxing, preparing themselves for the next session.

Your movements, punches, and foot patterns should follow a logical sequence and leave you in a balanced position, keeping in mind that all body and footwork movement needs to be free-flowing.

Jab and move

Throw smooth combinations

Constantly punch and move, making use of whatever floor space is available. Shadowboxing is also a great time to practice new combinations and review basic fundamentals. Visualize an opponent in front of you and perform the necessary moves, be it attacking or defending. Shadowboxing puts you in the ring with your opponent.

Shadowboxing Basics

Start by practicing your footwork moving in a variety of directions, remembering to stay light on your feet and maintaining a balanced boxing stance.

Keep your hands in the on-guard position when you are shadowboxing.

Throw a few jabs as you move into position to strike your imaginary opponent and then move around. Review the technicalities of your jab ensuring the movement is smooth and accurate. Continue to move in multiple directions throwing crisp jabs. As you become more comfortable with the single punches start to put two and three punch combinations together. Throw a jab, followed by a straight right. This is the classic 'one-two' combination. Focus on throwing the combination smoothly and always returning promptly to the on-guard position. This is a combination that you will return to over and over and is the starting point for many multiple punch combinations. Get creative and add variety to your punch combinations. Double up on your punches. Throw two fast jabs or two hooks consecutively. Visualize throwing punches to your opponent's body by bending your knees and lowering your body position. Throw a quick left jab or a 'one-two' combination to the body. Now rise up quickly and throw some punches in the direction of the head.

Focus on proper form. There is no benefit to throwing sloppy punches. Ensure you are executing all moves correctly to develop positive muscle memory. Punching speed and punching power will come later.

Punch Sequencing

Boxing coaches often work with simple number sequences to designate specific punch combinations. More detail will be given on number sequencing and punch combinations in the punch mitts chapter. It is however, a good time to start to practice with the number sequencing while you are shadowboxing. The jab is the most important punch and is always designated as 'one'. The straight right usually follows the jab and is designated as 'two'. The left hook is identified as 'three' and the right uppercut is known as 'four'.

As you execute a single punch, the movement should leave you in the correct position to deliver your next punch. If the first move puts you off balance slightly, the next move should bring you back on balance. An example of a combination that demonstrates the desired smooth transitional movements is a 'one-two-three' combination: a left jab, followed by a straight right and finishing with a left hook. Start this combination by throwing a quick left jab (one). Next your hips rotate as you pivot on your rear foot and a straight right is launched (two). This should now you leave you in position to throw a short, left hook (three). As you deliver the left hook, bring your hand back into the on-guard position, ready for your next punch. This simple three-punch combination teaches you to transfer your weight while pivoting on the balls of your feet and staying balanced. Practice this three-punch combination until you are proficient at it and then add on more punches.

Keep your combinations simple at first as you decide what punches you want to throw and the desired location of your punch. If you are having trouble with your punch combinations, slow down your punches slightly, throw fewer punches and focus on proper form.

KEYS TO SUCCESS

Bring your hands back to the on-guard position after every punch sequence.

—

Use the floor space, never standing in one place.

—

Maintain balance, timing your footwork with your punches.

DEFENSIVE MOVES

Mastering defensive moves is essential to be a successful boxer. For the *Ultimate Boxing Workout*, incorporating slips, ducks, and feints adds an element of realism to your shadowboxing training. Both core and leg muscles are also required to perform defensive moves, making shadowboxing an effective workout.

Slips

One way boxers avoid getting hit by punches is to 'slip' out of the way. Slipping utilizes a side-to-side motion of your head and upper body allowing evasion of an oncoming punch. Learning to slip effectively also allows boxers to stay in range to throw counterpunches of their own.

▼ Slip right

To slip punches, start with your hands up in the on-guard position and your body weight slightly forward, dip to the right or the left and immediately return to your original stance. Always keep your target in view. Although it is mostly an upper body move, the legs play an important role in slipping. Keep your knees bent and think of your legs as shock absorbers assisting in moving you quickly from side-to-side. Remain on the balls of your feet and do not lean back on your heels.

Incorporating slipping moves in between your punch combinations provides additional fitness benefits such as the use of your core muscles and the expenditure of more calories.

Visualize slipping a left jab

Visualize slipping a straight right

▼ Slip left

Slip a Left Jab

Visualize a left jab coming from your opponent and then dip to the right, by shifting your body to the right. Your right knee bends slightly. Keep your hands up.

Slip a Straight Right

Visualize a straight right coming from your opponent and then dip to the left, by shifting your body to the left. Your left knee bends slightly. Keep your hands up.

KEYS TO SUCCESS

Make sure you do not over slip by shifting your weight too much to one side. Stay centred over your feet.

—

Keep your hands close to your chin in the on-guard protective position when slipping.

Ducking

Another defensive move boxers use to avoid getting hit is called 'ducking'. Ducking, also known as 'bobbing and weaving', is used to avoid big powerful inside punches like hooks.

Starting in the balanced boxing stance, keep your back straight and bend both knees to 'drop' or lower your body in one quick motion. The motion is very similar to performing a quick squat. This is generally a small downward movement, not going any lower than 90 degrees at the knees. The idea is to duck just enough for the oncoming punch to safely go over the top of your head. Always return to your on-guard position as quickly as possible.

Incorporating ducking moves into your punching routine will give you a more effective workout, challenging the core muscles, gluteus, hamstrings, and quadriceps.

KEYS TO SUCCESS

Bend your knees to lower the body position. Bend at your waist only slightly.

—

Stay on the balls of your feet as you duck. Do not lean backward.

—

Keep ducking moves quick and concise.

—

Do not bend too low.

Feints

A feint is a calculated action or movement with the intent to deceive your opponent. By making your opponent think you are going to do one thing then doing another, opportunities are created to land punches. You can use shoulder and arm feints to confuse your opponent. Pretend to punch, but do not throw the punch. You can also use your feet to test your opponent's reaction by pretending to move in one direction, then move in another direction. Pretend to direct the punch to one region of the body and then go to a different part of the body. For example: Start by aiming your punch at the body region, but quickly redirect the punch to the head region. Feints should be subtle and not obvious.

Visualize ducking under a right hook

Feint with a left jab and throw a straight right

Shadowboxing with a virtual opponent

footwork and the punches together. Throw a multitude of punches working at a quick pace. Keep moving, using lateral movement, and staying on your toes. Make use of imagery to slip and duck your 'opponent's' punches. Shadowboxing at a fast pace for three-minute rounds will prepare your body for working on the punch mitts and on the heavy bag. Work hard enough so that you feel slightly out of breath, and ready and eager for more. Utilize the one-minute rest in between rounds to imagine new defensive scenarios and plan creative punch combinations. Always have a purpose when you shadowbox and vary the selection of your punches as you add slips and feints to your routine. Good boxers are never predictable. So mix it up!

MIRROR TRAINING

One of the best ways to perfect your punches and movement is to shadowbox in front of a mirror. You need a large mirror and sufficient space that allows you to punch and move freely. If a combination feels awkward and is not flowing you can check your performance in front of the mirror and make modifications. Are you holding your hands too low? Are your arms at the correct angle? Are you shifting your body weight properly and effortlessly?

Executing Basic Feints

Shoulder Feint: Jerk your left shoulder forward as though you are going to throw a jab, but throw a straight right instead.

Foot Feint: Half step with your front foot looking like you are moving left, step back circling to the right and then throw a left jab.

Punch Feint: Swiftly move just your right hand forward as if you are going to throw a straight right and then come back with a left hook.

Body Punch Feint: Bend your knees and drop down low in a position to throw a punch to the body region. Quickly rise up and throw a punch to the head region.

Remember you are trying to replicate a real fighting scenario. Adding feints to your punching routine while shadowboxing, working the punch mitts, and hitting the heavy bags makes for a more realistic boxing experience. If you want to watch a master at feinting, view fight-footage of the 'Hands of Stone', Roberto Duran.

KEYS TO SUCCESS

Keep the movement subtle. Do not over exaggerate your feints.

—

Practice in front of a large mirror to sharpen this skill and to ensure the movement is realistic.

—

Return your fists to the on-guard position quickly so that you are in the correct position to execute your punch.

Shadowboxing with a Virtual Opponent

Have a mental image of your opponent and what you want to achieve. Try to find a comfortable rhythm as you punch and move around matching the

Shadowboxing with weights

By studying your movement and punches in front of a mirror it is easier to make adjustments and change your execution and delivery. Throwing punches correctly allows for smooth transitions and reduces the chance of injuring your shoulder and elbow joints. Put time into practicing shadowboxing and mirror training to ensure an easy transition to working on the bags.

Improving Hand Speed

Once you have mastered your punches, practice your shadowboxing routine holding onto light hand weights, (1-1.5 kg; 2-3 lb). This added resistance makes it more of a challenge to keep your hands up and execute your punches. It also develops muscle strength and endurance in your shoulders and arms. Only use hand weights once you are completely warmed up and throw your punches no more than 70 per cent of your maximum punching power. Ensure you are executing the punches properly and have a secure grip on the weights. Do not use weights heavier than 1.5 kg (3 lb) as the excess load may increase the risk of injury to the ligaments and tendons of your shoulder joints.

After thoroughly warming up and completing one three-minute round

of shadowboxing without weights, perform one or two rounds while holding the hand weights. This will challenge you to keep your hands up high in the on-guard position and teach you to utilize proper punching technique. The arm and shoulder muscles are trained, resulting in improved muscular strength and endurance, giving you faster and more powerful punches.

Shadowboxing Combinations

1. **Double and triple jabs**
2. **'One-two':** *left jab followed by a straight right*
3. **'One-two-three':** *left jab, straight right, left hook*
4. **'One-two-three-four':** *left jab, straight right, left hook, right uppercut*
5. **Left jab-right uppercut-left hook**
6. **Left jab-left hook-straight right-left hook**
7. **Jab-jab-right:** *this is a double left jab followed by a straight right*
8. **Feint the left jab:** *throw a straight right – finish with a left hook*
9. **Left jab to the body:** *left jab to the head*
10. **'One–two':** *combination to the body, 'one–two' combination to the head*

Free Style Shadowboxing

Freestyle shadowboxing lets you practice all the punches and boxing moves. It allows you to get into the 'zone' and develop your own individual style. Since you are not wearing boxing gloves or striking a bag, your hands will never feel faster or lighter than when you are shadowboxing. As you become proficient with the classic shadowboxing combinations, start to improvise offensive and defensive moves, develop smooth transitions, and add slips, ducks, and feints. Your goal is to deliver fast paced punches that flow easily and allow you to slip and counterpunch your opponent's moves. Get in the zone by developing a boxer's mentality. Would you give any less than 100 per cent if you were facing a live opponent? Visualize doing battle in the ring, focus and give your best effort throughout the Ultimate Boxing Workout. Enjoy the freedom of movement and the opportunity to create countless punch combinations that will be limited only by your own imagination.

Freestyle shadowboxing

Basic Shadowboxing Drill
(1 – 3 minute round)
For this three-minute drill you will need a training partner to call out some basic punch combinations and motivate you. As the round starts have your hands in the on-guard position, keep moving continuously, and be ready to respond as your partner calls out single and multiple punch combinations. When your partner calls 'one', throw a left jab. When your partner calls 'two', throw a straight right. When your partner calls 'three', throw a left hook and when your partner calls 'four', throw a right uppercut. Always bring your hands quickly back to the on-guard position, move around and prepare for the next call. Next, start to work on punch combinations. When a 'one-two' is called, throw a left jab, followed by a straight right. For a 'one-two-three', throw a left jab, straight right, and then a left hook. 'One-two-three-four', throw a left jab, straight right, left hook, and end with a right uppercut. When calling out punch sequences for your partner ensure there is adequate time for the puncher to move around between punch combinations. This exercise will teach you to react quickly and improve your response time.

Punch Sequencing Summary

'One': *jab*
'Two': *straight right*
'Three': *left hook*
'Four': *right uppercut*
'One-two': *jab-straight right*
'One-two-three': *jab-straight right-left hook*
'One-two-three-four': *jab-straight right-left hook-right uppercut*

Always remember to return your hands to the on-guard position and keep moving around until your partner calls the next sequence. When it is your turn to call the punch sequence for your partner call out plenty of single jabs. Remember the jab should be the most frequently thrown punch. The purpose of this drill is to continuously punch and move, gradually building punch combinations.

Hand Speed Drill
(Intermediate to Advanced)
Champion boxers will often throw more than 200 punches in a 3-minute round. The hand speed drill gives you a sense of what it is like to throw multiple rapid-fire punches and is a conditioning drill that will definitely increase your heart rate quite quickly. It is important to be aware of proper punch execution at all time. Successful boxers condition themselves by constantly throwing punch after punch. You will require a timer to execute this drill.

For one minute, throw 10 punch-flurries as fast as you can with a two-second break. During the two-second break, remember to take deep breaths, reset, and move for your next series of punches. Aim to repeat this a total of ten times in a minute.

When the minute is up, take a 20-second rest before starting your second minute punch-flurry circuit. Aim to throw 100 punches in one-minute. Take another 20-second rest and finish with a third round. Breathe naturally while throwing all of your punches and always ensure that you are not holding your breath. If you finish your 100 punches in under a minute just keep moving and jabbing until the minute is up. Focus on working multiple combinations throwing all your punches at full blast. During the 20-second rest perform shoulder circles to loosen up your shoulders and back.

Perform this drill only after you are thoroughly warmed up.

Circuit 1 (1 minute)
10 sets of 10 punches
Rest - 20 seconds
Circuit 2 (1 minute)
10 sets of 10 punches
Rest - 20 seconds
Circuit 3 (1 minute)
10 sets of 10 punches
Rest - 20 seconds

Light Hand Weights
Depending on your conditioning level you can increase the difficulty level by holding onto hand weights. Since this is an intense punching drill use no more than 1 kg (2 lb) hand weights and remember to throw your punches at 70 per cent.

Never underestimate the importance of shadowboxing, not just as a warm-up or as a cool down, but as an important component of your Ultimate Boxing Workout.

▼ Shadowboxing drill

PROTECTING YOUR HANDS

Protecting your hands should be one of your highest priorities when performing a boxing workout. Properly wrapping your hands and utilizing quality gloves is the place to start.

Hand Wraps
The purpose of hand wrapping is to protect the bones, joints, and ligaments in your hands, to give additional support to your wrists, and to avoid cuts to your knuckles. These reusable protective wraps reduce the chance of both short-term and long-term damage and discomfort to your hands.

There are basically two different styles of hand wraps. Mexican style hand wraps are generally a blend of spandex and semi-elastic cotton that allows for a superior fit. Traditional hand wraps are made of a cotton woven material that tends to bunch and become heavy when your hands sweat.

Hand wraps are available in various lengths, 400 to 450 cm (160 to 180 in). If your hand wraps are too short you will be unable to wrap your hands effectively and thoroughly for protection. We recommend using the longer hand wraps at 450 cm (180 inch). Also look for wraps with a wide Velcro closure for a more secure fit and durability.

There are many different techniques for wrapping your hands, each ritualistic to the individual. Some may want more wrap coverage around the knuckle area and others may want more wrap support on the wrist area. Listed below is an effective hand wrapping method.

Basic Hand Wrapping Technique

STEP 1
With a relaxed open hand, spread your fingers wide. Place loop of the hand wrap around the thumb with the wrap falling to the front side of the hand.

STEP 2
Wrap twice around the wrist.

STEP 3
Wrap once around the thumb. Always wrap in the direction away from the body.

STEP 4

Wrap around the knuckles three or four times and make sure you keep your fingers spread wide. Make a fist often to check that the tension of the hand wrap is not too tight. Overlap the side edges of the wrap slightly, keeping it flat.

STEP 5

Bring the wrap to the base of the thumb using it as the anchor. Pull the wrap between the small finger and the ring finger.

STEP 6

Return the wrap to the base of the thumb and pull it between the ring finger and the long finger.

STEP 7

Return to the base of the thumb once again and pull the wrap between the long finger and the index finger and then back to the wrist.

STEP 8

From the wrist take the wrap to the knuckles and wrap a few more times.

STEP 9

With the remainder, continue to wrap around the wrist and hand in a figure-eight pattern. Pull the wrap in front and down toward the wrist.

STEP 10

Wrap under the wrist and up over the front of the hand to finish the second part of the figure-eight pattern. Repeat several times.

STEP 11

Leave sufficient wrap to finish around the wrist a few times. Secure with the Velcro fastener.

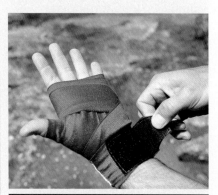

IT IS IMPORTANT TO WRAP WITH AN EVEN TENSION. THE WRAP SHOULD FEEL SNUG ENOUGH TO GIVE SUFFICIENT SUPPORT, BUT NOT SO TIGHT THAT YOUR HAND CIRCULATION IS COMPROMISED. WHEN YOU ARE TRAINING, ALWAYS WEAR YOUR HAND WRAPS UNDER YOUR GLOVES TO PROTECT YOUR HANDS, KNUCKLES, AND WRISTS.

CHAPTER TWO

▼ Heavy bag gloves

▼ Sparring gloves

GLOVES

There are essentially three types of gloves: boxing gloves, sparring gloves, and heavy bag gloves. Boxing gloves are used in competitive matches and are secured by laces. Sparring gloves are used for sparring and training drills and can either have Velcro fasteners or laces. Heavy bag gloves are used to hit the bags and punch mitts. They are secured with Velcro fasteners. Heavy bag gloves are designed to hold up to the wear and tear of hitting a heavy bag versus hitting an opponent. For the Ultimate Boxing Workout you will require a quality pair of heavy bag gloves.

Gloves should be used specifically for what they are designed for and bag gloves should not be used for sparring or boxing.

Heavy Bag Gloves

When working the bags and the punch mitts, heavy bag gloves are your best choice. The gloves give extra protection for your hands, wrists, and knuckles. Ensure there is adequate space inside the gloves when your hands are wrapped, allowing for sufficient blood circulation. The gloves need to be snug around your hands, provide a comfortable fit and feel secure. Velcro fasteners provide extra support for the wrists and make it easy to put the gloves on and off quickly. They are generally made out of leather or synthetic materials. Many of the higher quality gloves also have sweat wicking properties inside of the glove.

Personal preference will dictate the weight of the glove you choose, ranging from 10 ounces to 16 ounces. It is essential that your gloves feel comfortable and have sufficient padding to absorb the impact of hitting the heavy bag.

JUMP ROPE WORKOUTS

JUMP ROPE TRAINING OR SKIPPING IS ONE OF THE BEST TOTAL BODY WORKOUTS AND ENGAGES ALMOST EVERY MUSCLE IN THE BODY. TRAINING FOR OTHER SPORTS LIKE TENNIS, SOCCER, FOOTBALL, ICE HOCKEY, OR THE 'WARRIOR-STYLE' OBSTACLE COURSE RACES ACQUIRE MAJOR BENEFITS FROM JUMP ROPE TRAINING.

According to the British Rope Skipping Association, 10-minutes of vigorous skipping can have the similar health benefits as a 45-minute run. Jump rope is an effective method for improving speed, coordination, agility, and dynamic balance. It improves eye/hand/foot coordination, timing, fluidity, and lateral movement. It engages the legs for jumping, the abdominals for stabilization, uses the arms and shoulders to manoeuvre the rope and the forearms to generate the rope speed.

A professor at Louisiana State University's Biomedical Research Center, Tim Church, states; "Boxers jump rope because the precise timing it requires between the feet and hands helps connect the upper and lower body with the brain. One of the benefits of jumping rope is that the intensity you work at can be as high as you want it to be."

Getting Started

Jumping rope is a great portable workout and you can practically jump anywhere, indoors or outside. With practice and commitment, the basic jumps can be mastered and then a wide variety of combinations can be performed. Not only does jumping rope improve cardiovascular endurance, it will also provide significant gains in the performance level for virtually every sport.

TYPES OF ROPES

There are many types of ropes available to purchase, ranging from plastic ropes, beaded ropes, nylon ropes, leather ropes to weighted ropes. Quality leather and plastic ropes permit a fast pace and allow for rope manoeuvrability. A plastic beaded or segmented jump rope allows you to adjust the length of the rope and customize it specifically for your needs. Nylon ropes tend to be too light making it difficult to create a sufficient amount of momentum to produce the desired motion or arc.

Weighted ropes often produce heavy, slow, awkward rotations and place additional stress on the wrists, forearms, and shoulders. The desired outcome of jumping is to develop cardiovascular fitness, fluidity, and agility. A rope that is too heavy or too light defeats this purpose and may take away from your ability to concentrate on proper jumping form and technique.

Select a rope that allows for a sufficient arc and does not place additional stress on the forearms and wrists. Also, choose a rope with handles that allow for easy rotation of the rope and fit comfortably into your hands.

▼ Proper Rope Length

Proper Rope Length

To choose which rope length is best for you, hold the handles of the rope in each hand and stand with one foot on the middle of the rope. Pull the rope up tight. The rope handles should reach the upper chest area. Using a rope that is the correct length will make it easier to execute your jumps.

Stick With It

For even the most well-conditioned athlete, jumping rope can be a humbling experience. Finding a consistent, rhythmic pace comes easily for some, while others have more difficulty. Everyone has a different learning curve and with the right attitude and motivation anyone can learn to jump rope within a few sessions.

How to Jump

Basic tips to get you started.

- Stand with your feet side-by-side, hip width apart, and your knees slightly bent.
- Hold the handles firmly, (without squeezing), in your hands with your elbows bent slightly at the sides of your body.
- Start with the rope behind your feet.
- Keep the neck and shoulders relaxed and hold the head in a neutral position.
- Initiate the turning of the rope at your wrists. The shoulders and arms stay relaxed with little movement.
- Turn the rope smoothly.
- Push off the floor into the air with both feet.
- For the basic manoeuvres, your feet will only come 6 to 10 cm (2 to 3 in) off of the floor.
- Land softly on the floor and roll through the balls of the feet to help absorb the impact.
- The body remains upright and does not lean forward or backward.
- To reduce stress on the feet and legs, jump on a wood sprung floor.
- Always focus on proper technique.

The Neutral Move

The neutral move can be incorporated into your jump rope training if you are still developing your timing, trying more difficult jumps, or working on new foot patterns. Also known as side-rope swings, the neutral moves can help minimize the frustration of stopping and starting, and allows you to train continuously.

▼ Push off the floor with both feet into the air

▲ Neutral move – Place both handles in one hand

Place both handles in one hand and rotate the rope in a forward motion at the side of the body. Ensure the rope stays at the side of the body and does not cross or wander in front. Maintain the proper position of the shoulders, arms, and wrists. Turn the rope with your wrist and forearm with the same motion as when you are actually jumping through the rope. Now you can perform the new jump sequences or foot patterns, focusing on your footwork and timing without worrying about catching the rope on your feet. Switch the rope to the opposite hand to add variety. Once you have mastered the new jump or foot pattern, hold the handles in each hand and perform them jumping through the rope.

EVERYONE HAS A DIFFERENT LEARNING CURVE AND WITH THE RIGHT ATTITUDE AND MOTIVATION ANYONE CAN LEARN TO JUMP ROPE WITHIN A FEW SESSIONS

You can also use the neutral move when a short rest is required. Place both handles in one hand, turning the rope at the side of the body and keeping the feet moving by marching on the spot. Catch your breath and then return to your jumps. Eventually you can reduce the amount of time resting and continue jumping as your cardiovascular endurance improves.

JUMP ROPE PROGRESSIONS

Basic, intermediate, and advanced jumps are described below. With each training session, you will notice that your timing improves and you have more endurance. Continue to work on the basic jumps and then try adding some new combinations.

BASIC JUMPS

Basic Two-Foot Jump

The basic two-foot jump is your baseline for more complex jumps and footwork. This is the most common jump rope technique and is also known as the 'bounce step' or 'one hop'. Keep both feet together while you jump in the air, one jump for each revolution of the rope. Start with your feet side by side and the rope behind your feet. Push off the ground with both feet, while keeping the shoulders and neck relaxed, and the head facing forward.

▼ Basic Two-Foot Jump

▲ Boxer's skip (close up)

▼ Two Foot bounce forward

Keep both arms by the sides of the body, rotating the rope at the wrists. Rotate the rope upward and forward over your head, in front of the body, and down to the floor and under your feet. Land on the balls of your feet allowing your knees to bend slightly to absorb the landing impact. To keep the jump efficient and effective, jump fairly close to the floor, 2 to 4 cm (1 to 2 in). By increasing the speed of the rope rotation, the intensity of jump will increase. You will find this basic two-foot jump the easiest to master.

Boxer's Skip
The boxer's skip involves shifting your weight slightly from one foot to the other with each jump. The shift in weight is subtle as both feet are still making contact with the floor. You can perform a single bounce — right foot, left foot, or a double bounce — two rights, two lefts. This is a move up from the basic two-foot jump and lays the groundwork for more difficult jumps. Relax the shoulders and neck and remember to jump just a few centimetres off of the floor.

Forward and Backward Bounce
Keep your feet together and jump forward and then backward, travelling about 10 cm (4 in) or more. Increase your jump distance by pushing off the floor with more power. Always ensure that the natural arc of the rope is maintained. Perform the basic two-foot jump several times to set your rhythm.

Kick-Step
The kick-step involves a slight kick forward alternating with each leg. Start with the boxer's skip, lift the right foot

▼ Kick-Step (A-B)

A

Kick-Step – start

slightly backward and then perform a small kick forward. After the kick, land on the right foot. Now, lift the left foot slightly backward and kick it forward, landing on the left foot. Alternate the kicking legs and increase the difficulty by travelling forward and backward as you perform the kick-step.

INTERMEDIATE JUMPS
High Knee Jog

Similar to running on the spot, alternate lifting your knees high in front. Keep the body upright and the arms in the correct position. Land softly on the ground, using the feet, knees, and legs to absorb the impact. By lifting the knees high, the intensity level of the workout increases. Start this cardio interval training session by performing 8-10 high knee lifts and then take it down to a boxer's skip to recover. Repeat the high knee jog, increasing the numbers of knee lifts as you become more proficient. If you are trying

START THIS CARDIO INTERVAL TRAINING SESSION BY PERFORMING 8-10 HIGH KNEE LIFTS AND THEN TAKE IT DOWN TO A BOXER'S SKIP TO RECOVER

to work this jump into your routine, you can add high knee lifts travelling forward and backward. This jump develops the muscle power in your legs and challenges your cardiovascular system.

Lateral Hops

Jump with both feet together like the basic two-foot jump. As the rope rotates, jump to the right and then to the left, back and forth, for a distance of about a 30 cm (12 in). A slight rope

▼ High Knee Jog (A-B)

B

Kick-Step – finish

A

High Knee Jog – start

B

High Knee Jog – finish

▼ Lateral Hops (A-B)

A

adjustment has to be made as well, since your body is moving side to side. This jump is more challenging since your feet are moving out of the centre position and the rope can easily get tangled with your feet. When performing this side-to-side jump, you will find that your arms have a tendency to travel outward, so focus on keeping your elbows by the sides of the body. Try to complete 4 – 6 lateral hops and then go back to the basic skip. Increase the number of lateral hops as you become more proficient.

The Boxer's Shuffle

The boxer's shuffle pays tribute to the classic Muhammad Ali foot movement utilized to confuse opponents. While moving around the ring Ali would suddenly shuffle his feet forward and backward, and then throw an unexpected series of punches. Practicing this jump will train you to stay light

B

▼ Boxer's Shuffle (A-B-C)

B

A

C

▼ Jumpin Jacks (A-B)

A

B

on your feet and ready for any directional changes. The shifting of your foot positioning will also challenge your balance skills.

This is how to perform a slightly slower version of the shuffle. Jump in the air, moving one foot slightly forward and the other foot slightly backward, and then land on the floor with both feet at the same time. Push off the floor again, taking the front foot toward the back and the back foot toward the front. Land with both feet on the floor alternating your feet constantly. Repeat, moving quickly and landing softly. Your agility and response time will be challenged due to the quick movement of the feet moving forward and backward. Complete 8 – 10 shuffles, then return to the boxer's skip.

Jumping Jacks

Jumping jacks are old school calisthenics and can easily be worked into your rope training. As you jump, separate your feet shoulder-width apart. Land softly through the feet and then jump again bringing the feet together to land. Repeat. When performing this jump be careful not to make the foot separation too wide as the rope will most likely get tangled with your feet. Start out with 6- 8 jumping jacks and increase the number as you become more proficient.

Criss-Cross Feet

This jump has a similar foot pattern to jumping jacks but requires more timing and concentration. Jump with your feet about shoulder-width apart. As you jump again bring the legs in and land with the feet in this crossed position. Jump again, taking the feet wide and landing with a two-foot jump. Jump again, bringing the other foot in front and landing in a crossed foot position and repeat. You may find this more challenging than the jumping jack as the crossed feet can put you off balance. If you are having difficulty with this jump practice the footwork without a rope.

AS YOU JUMP AGAIN BRING THE LEGS IN AND LAND WITH THE FEET IN THIS CROSSED POSITION. JUMP AGAIN, TAKING THE FEET WIDE AND LANDING WITH A TWO-FOOT JUMP.

▲ Criss-Cross Feet

ADVANCED JUMPS
Double Jumps

To perform double jumps, jump high enough to allow two rotations of the rope while you are in the air. The rope speed must be faster and the jump must be substantially higher than the basic jump. Set your rhythm by performing a few basic two-foot jumps or boxer's skips, and then perform a magnified jump with two fast rotations of the rope. As your timing and your fitness

TO PERFORM DOUBLE JUMPS, JUMP HIGH ENOUGH TO ALLOW TWO ROTATIONS OF THE ROPE WHILE YOU ARE IN THE AIR.

▲ Double Jumps

level improves, reduce the number of basic jumps in between your double jumps. This demanding jump requires more leg power and increased rope speed to be successful. Double jumps or double hops, will improve your cardio-fitness and muscular endurance. Try to perform 6 double jumps working your way up to 15.

▼ Crossovers (A-B-C)

Crossovers

Perform a basic jump at a comfortable pace. When the rope is overhead and moving forward, cross your arms at waist level and jump through the rope. When crossing the arms keep the handles by the sides of the body with the left handle at the right hip and the right handle at the left hip. The second time the rope comes overhead uncross the arms and jump through the rope once again. Keep the rope handles pointing out to the sides and not downward. When you perform the arm crossover motion you will have to jump slightly higher than the basic jump. Try to complete three to four front rope-cross jumps interspersed with a few basic or boxer's skip in between. Work up to 8 to 10 front crossovers in a row. This jump is also called a front rope-cross.

▼ Reverse Rope Jump

▼ Jumping Jack-Knee Lift (A-B)

A

B

Reverse Rope Jump

Start the reverse jump with the boxer's skip and rotating the rope in a backward direction. The rope starts in front of the feet, not behind the feet. It is important to keep your hands and arms in the correct position by the sides of the body and not allow them to lift up and away from the sides.

Combination Jumps

Combining foot patterns adds an element of interest and difficulty.

Combo Jump #1

Jumping Jack-Knee Lift

This combination starts with performing one jumping jack. Jump opening the feet wide and land on the floor. Jump again to bring the feet together and land on the floor. Jump and lift one knee up while hopping on the other foot. Land on both feet and perform the next jumping jack. Repeat lifting the other knee. To transition from the jumping jack to the high knee lift perform a basic two-foot jump.

Combo Jump # 2
Boxer's Shuffle and Jumping Jacks
Combining the Boxer's Shuffle with Jumping Jacks will assist you in improving balance, timing, and agility. Perform eight boxer's shuffles, then eight jumping jacks. To transition from the shuffle to the jack, perform a basic two-foot jump. Shuffle-shuffle-basic-jack. Decrease down to a single shuffle, basic jump and a single jack.

Freestyle Jumping
Your goal is to jump in a freestyle manner, incorporating a wide variety of moves and foot patterns into your skipping routine. Develop a smooth

▼ Boxer's Shuffle and Jumping Jacks (A-B)

▼ Freestyle Jumping

rhythm. There are a countless number of jump patterns you can perform, but to get there you need to focus on the basics. Work the fundamentals before trying more complicated jumps and then use the neutral move to develop your new combinations. No matter how long you decide to jump, make it fun and challenging.

JUMP ROPE WORKOUTS

Boxing is an interval training method that follows a pattern of three-minutes of hard work, followed by one-minute of rest. You can choose to adopt this same training format when jumping rope. Three minutes of jumping followed by one minute of rest is a great way to work up to jumping for 10 to 15 minutes continuously.

Warm up before starting to jump by shadowboxing for 2 to 3 minutes. Warm up the shoulder, core, and legs muscle by moving across the floor, punching, ducking, and slipping.

BASIC INTERVAL WORKOUT
Boxer's Skip - *1 minute*
Kick Step - *30 seconds*
Boxer's Skip - *30 seconds*
High Knee Jog - *15 seconds*
Boxer's Skip - *30 seconds*
Front & Back Bounce - *15 seconds*
Boxer's Skip - *1 minute*

You can choose to repeat the interval 2 to 3 times. Take a one-minute rest break in between intervals.

INTERMEDIATE INTERVAL WORKOUT
Boxer's Skip - *2 minutes*
High Knees - *15 seconds*
Boxer's Skip - *30 seconds*
Jumping Jacks - *15 seconds*
Boxer's Skip - *30 seconds*
Boxer's Shuffle - *15 seconds*
Boxer's Skip - *30 seconds*
High Knees Sprint - *30 seconds*
Boxer's Skip - *1 minute*

You can choose to repeat the interval 2 to 3 times. Take a one-minute rest break in between intervals.

▼ Intermediate Interval Workout

ADVANCED INTERVAL WORKOUT
Boxer's Skip - *1 minute*
High Knee Jog - *30 seconds*
Boxer's Skip - *30 seconds*
Scissors - *30 seconds*
Boxer's Skip - *30 seconds*
Lateral Jumps - *30 seconds*
Boxer's Skip - *30 seconds*
Double Jumps - *15 seconds*
Boxer's Skip - *30 seconds*
Double Jumps - *15 seconds*
Boxer's Skip - *2 minutes*

You can choose to repeat the interval 2 to 3 times. Take a one-minute rest break in between intervals.

Jump Rope Sprints

This is an advanced, interval routine, placing demands on your shoulders, core muscles, arms, and the cardiovascular system. Skip as fast as you can for short, timed intervals.

Option One: Jump as fast as possible for 30 seconds and then rest for 30 seconds. Repeat for 10 to 15 sets. This drill should take you approximately 15 minutes to complete 15 sets. During the rest phase, walk around, keep moving, and catch your breath. To make this drill more challenging jump as fast as possible for 30 seconds and reduce the rest time between sprints.

Option Two: Perform a 30-second sprint followed by jumping with the rope at a lower intensity for 30 seconds. Repeat for 6 to 10 sets.

It is best to choose a simple foot pattern you are comfortable with and can perform at a very fast pace. Once you become more proficient with the simple jumps incorporate more challenging moves like crossovers or double jumps for your sprints.

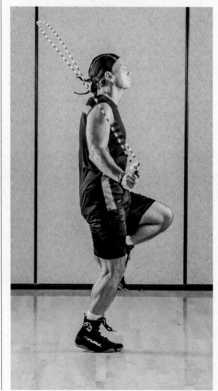

Jump Rope Ladders

This interval drill helps to build your jumping stamina. Choose a number of jumps to start. For example, set a goal of 400 jumps, maintaining a consistent jumping pace. Take a 30 to 60-second rest. Reduce the number of jumps by 50 for each set. For your next ladder, jump 350 times, then take a 30 to 60-second rest. Continue the down ladder to 50 jumps taking a 30 to 60-second rests in between. During the rest periods keep moving around.

▲ Jump Rope Ladders

JUMP	REST
400	*30 - 60 seconds*
350	*30 - 60 seconds*
300	*30 - 60 seconds*
250	*30 - 60 seconds*
200	*30 - 60 seconds*
150	*30 - 60 seconds*
100	*30 - 60 seconds*
50	*30 - 60 seconds*

The total number of jumps you will perform is 1,800 for the 8 sets. This should take about 14 minutes if you are resting for 30 seconds and about 18 minutes to complete, assuming you are resting for a full minute. To increase difficulty, take shorter rest periods between the sets or choose a higher starting number. Initially you may want to start your ladder at 300 jumps and reduce by 50 jumps each set, to the last 50 jumps.

KEYS TO SUCCESS

Select the correct length of rope for your height.

—

Perform one jump for each rotation of the rope.

—

Ensure the rotation of the rope is moving at a constant speed.

—

When turning the rope keep the arms by the sides of your body.

—

Perfect your foot timing by practicing the basic jumps.

—

Incorporate the neutral move when putting together new jump combinations.

—

Move around. Boxers never stay in one place.

The speed of the rope rotations, your height, body type, fitness level, and experience will influence the number of jumps performed. A starting jumping pace is around 110 to 130 per minute, an intermediate jumping pace is between 130 to 150 per minute, and a more advanced pace is about 160 to 180 jumps per minute. Listen to motivating music, warm up thoroughly and just start jumping. We will show you how to incorporate jump rope into a complete Ultimate Boxing Workout in Chapter 10, The Boxing Interval Training System, (B.I.T.S.).

The Champ, Floyd Mayweather Jr.

PUNCHING BAG WORKOUTS

THE FOUNDATIONS OF A BOXING WORKOUT ARE TIED TO WORKING THE BAGS. THERE IS NO MORE DYNAMIC TRAINING EXPERIENCE THAN THIS. THE SIMPLICITY IN THE DESIGN AND EFFECTIVENESS OF THE HEAVY BAG, SPEED BAG, AND DOUBLE-END BAG MAKES THIS 'OLD SCHOOL' TRAINING EQUIPMENT TIMELESS. THESE ARE THE FOUNDATION OF A BOXING WORKOUT.

Virtual Opponent

The heavy bag is your opponent. There is really no other way to look at it. Treat it with respect, like a dangerous challenger that can strike you at any time. Remember the sport we are trying to emulate is boxing, so visualization is extremely important. Move and throw punches on the bag as though you have a real live opponent in front of you. Warm up properly and prepare to go into battle with your virtual opponent, the heavy bag.

Hitting the Heavy Bag

There is an old saying in boxing 'nothing stays still in the ring'. When working the heavy bag constantly move, slip, and duck while throwing punch

Working out on the bags provides immediate feedback on your technique, ability, and punching power. Striking the larger bags provide an immense release of tension and improves muscular strength and endurance. Hitting the smaller bags develops quickness and eye-hand coordination, as well as tests and develops your agility and reaction time.

Boxing training equipment has evolved and today there are a few more bags available to train on, like a water filled bag and hook and uppercut wall mounted bag.

LARGE PUNCHING BAGS

HEAVY BAG

The heavy bag has legendary status as one of the most important pieces of apparatus to get you into the best shape ever. A great spontaneous creativity develops when hitting the heavy bag, with an endless number of punch combinations available. It is an exceptional workout that challenges your aerobic, anaerobic, and musculature systems.

The heavy bag is your opponent

▼ Hitting the heavy bag

Throw punches with precision, passion and purpose

"Sometimes I just like to focus on the technique and get it done as perfectly as possible. Then sometimes you just want to hit the bag as hard as you can and beat it up," says Cecilia Braekhus, Female World Welterweight Champion.

HEAVY BAG BASICS

Boxing Stance

After properly wrapping your hands and putting on your gloves, establish your boxing stance in front of the bag. Fully extend your left arm to make contact with the knuckle portion of your glove on the bag. Keep the wrist straight. Take a step back, moving 15 cm (6 in) away from the bag. This is the starting distance for working the bag and throwing punches. The moment your fist makes contact with the heavy bag, tighten your fist. Keep the hands in a semi-relaxed fist as you move around the bag. You will waste energy if you constantly hold your fist tight and stay too tense.

▼ Boxing Stance

Cecilia Braekhus

combinations. Work the bag as though you are competing in the boxing ring and throw punches with precision, passion, and purpose.

The time you have put into your shadowboxing and mirror training, as well as practicing the fundamentals will benefit your transition to the heavy bag.

▼ Range

Range

Be aware of your distance from the heavy bag and stay slightly more than an arm's length away. Your left jab is your range finder and it will give you a sense of how close you have to be to land other punches. Your straight punches will set up the short punches, such as hooks and uppercuts. Move your feet to get into range to strike the bag.

Throwing a left jab

Create Space

Determine your maximum punching distance. Throw some jabs ensuring your arm is fully extended as your glove makes contact with the centre of the bag. Make sure you are not standing too close to the bag keeping a realistic distance from your virtual or imaginary opponent. The aim is to maintain a consistent distance between you and the heavy bag.

Proper Punching Technique

Focus on throwing crisp punches aiming to hit the centre of the bag. When throwing jabs and straight rights, your arms should be almost fully extended upon impact. As soon as your glove makes impact with the bag, quickly return your fists to the on-guard position ready to throw your next punch. Your punch should jolt the bag with a quick, snapping motion. If you leave the punch out there too long, you are pushing the bag resulting in a sloppy, lazy punch. Keep your neck, shoulders, and arms relaxed and this will assist in throwing fast, snapping punches. 'Lead with speed, follow with power.' Never sacrifice technique for

Your left jab is your range finder

Straight right

Left hook to the mid section of the bag

Right uppercut on the heavy bag

Bend your knees to throw body punches

punching power. Start by throwing light, quick punches, gradually adding more power and use your imagination as you build two and three punch combinations.

'Punch and Get Out'

As you continue to establish your range and move around the bag, step forward with your punches and then step backward. This is called, 'Punch and Get Out'. At the moment of impact, keep your core muscles tight and return your hands to the on-guard position quickly. Pivot on the balls of your feet when throwing punches to maintain balance. This provides a stable stance from which maximum power can be executed. Never stand flat-footed and always stay on the balls of your feet ready to move in any direction. Once you have found your range with your left jab, try throwing some straight rights, and one-two combinations.

▼ Natural Swinging Motion

Punch and get out

Keep moving

Natural Swinging Motion

Incorporate the slight swinging motion of the bag into your punching rhythm as the heavy bag will swing in a natural motion when it is hit properly. You want to use this motion to time your punches while you move around the bag. A technically correct crisp punch will jolt the bag but not make it move excessively. Coordinate your footwork with the swinging motion of the bag and time your strikes by ensuring that your punches make solid contact with the bag as it comes toward you. Pushing your punches and not snapping them will create unnecessary swinging of the bag. Throwing wild punches or whaling at the bag as it is moving away will also cause the bag to swing uncontrollably, and you will never develop a good rhythm.

Keep Moving

Find a consistent punching pace that you can continue with and persevere to the end of the round. Keep up a steady punching pace for the entire three minutes of every round and use your one-minute rest to recover between rounds. When performing this type of interval training, you may have the tendency to hit the bag vigorously for the first 30 to 40 seconds and then be too winded to continue punching for the remainder of round. Remember to pace yourself.

Breathe Naturally

The body tenses up while punching the heavy bag and there is often a tendency to hold your breath for a split second. Stay relaxed and exhale as you throw your punches, then breathe in to get a new supply of oxygen to your working muscles. To perform any type of aerobic activity, proper exhalation is important. Find a natural breathing rhythm that suits you. Exhale on exertion and then inhale to replenish the oxygen to the body.

Breathe naturally

Left hook on the heavy bag

QnXINGSOURCE.COM

"Punches in bunches"

Mix It Up

Vary the tempo, speed, and selection of your punch combinations. Visualize punches coming at you from an opponent, slip or duck, and then counter with your own punches. Slipping and ducking helps you develop torso strength and improves your balance. Make sure you are not just targeting the head area. Throw some body punches into the mix. Set up your hooks and uppercuts with your straight punches. Then, move into position, throw your power shots and move out. Stay busy, find a smooth rhythm, and throw 'punches in bunches'.

KEYS TO SUCCESS

Focus on proper execution and punching technique.

—

Establish a realistic distance from the bag, slightly more than a jabs distance away. Your arm should be almost fully extended on impact when throwing straight punches.

—

Nothing stays still in the ring. Make sure you move around while throwing punches.

—

Snap your punches to avoid excessive swing of the heavy bag. Time your punches to make contact with the bag as it moves slightly toward you.

—

Do not drop your hands after punching. This will leave you out of position for your next series of punches.

Visualize slipping a left jab

Blocking punches

DEFENSIVE MOVES

Add slipping and ducking moves into your heavy bag punching combinations will challenge your core and leg muscles. These defensive moves add another level of realism and intensity to your boxing workout.

Visualize ducking under a left hook

Slipping

The slipping movement engages the core muscles of the torso. With your hands in the protective position imagine your opponent throwing a left jab. Slip the punch by dipping to your right making sure your eyes are always on your opponent. After slipping you can counter with a right to the body. Slip a straight right by bending your knees and lowering your body to the left. Counter by throwing a left hook.

Ducking

Ducking is another defensive move that provides fitness benefits. Ducking involves engagement of the gluteals, quadriceps and core muscles. By using your legs to lower your body and move under a punch, the body shifts from one side to the other. When you duck under a punch to the left counter back with a left hook, and when you duck under and over to the right counter with a right hook.

Blocking

There is no real fitness benefit to blocking, but it does help create actual combat scenarios. Keeping your hands up high in the on-guard position, your core muscles tight, and your gloves against your head, imagine your opponent throwing a left hook. Block the punch with your right glove. You can throw a left hook counter punch to the bag. Blocking a straight right from your opponent with your left glove, will allow you to counter with a right uppercut to the body.

Visualization

As mentioned, visualizing an opponent keeps the workout interesting and will motivate you to work harder. Some of these defensive moves will also be featured in the focus mitt drills (Chapter 5).

Visualize your opponent

VISUALIZING AN OPPONENT KEEPS THE WORKOUT INTERESTING AND WILL MOTIVATE YOU TO WORK HARDER

HEAVY BAG PUNCH COMBINATIONS

Basic Combinations
Double and Triple Jabs
Throw two or three rapid-fire jabs. Focus on speed not power when throwing double and triple jabs. Execute a stronger first jab and follow with the second or third jab by flicking fast and light with no pause between the jabs. The second and third jabs are executed by pulling back approximately one-third the distance of the first jab. It is all about speed, moving your opponent off-balance, and setting up to throw more powerful punches.

Jab to the Body – Jab to the Head
Lower your body position and step forward as you launch a quick left jab to the body, (dead centre just below the mid-portion of the bag).

Heavy bag combinations

Now raise your body position and immediately launch a jab to the head region. After you land your second jab, quickly step away from the bag ready to throw your next combination.

The One-Two

Throw a fast left jab followed immediately by a powerful straight right, returning both hands quickly to the on-guard position. Move away from the bag ready to throw your next combination. Throw one-two's to the head and one-two's to the body. To throw a one-two combination to the body, bend your legs to lower your position and aim your punches to the mid-section of the bag. Ensure your hands are in the correct on-guard position. This classic punch sequence is utilized more than any other combination.

One-Two Hook

Move forward as you launch a quick one-two combination, (left jab, straight right). You should now be in position to throw a short, left hook to complete the combination. Move away from the bag and get ready to throw your next punch sequence.

Basic Five Punch Combo - Double Jab to the Body - Single Jab to the Head - Straight Right – Left Hook

Lower your body throwing two quick, light jabs to the mid-section of the bag. Move up and throw a hard jab to the head, followed by a straight right to the head. Pivot and throw a short, left hook to the head.

Slip Combo - Jab to the Head – Slip Right – Straight Right – Left Hook to the Body

Lead with a left jab to the head. Visualize a left jab coming from your opponent and slip to the right. Immediately come back with a straight right to the head and dig in with a left hook to the body. Make sure your hands are up when you slip, remembering to pivot on the balls of your feet shifting your weight to add power to your punches.

Jab — Right Uppercut — Left Hook — Short Right Hand

Fire a left jab to the head, move forward and throw a right uppercut to the body, followed by a left hook to the head and then finish with a short right to the head.

Intermediate/Advanced Combinations

One-Two - Double Left Hook

Lower your body position and throw a quick one-two to the mid-section. Follow up with a fast left hook to the body and immediately rise up and throw your second left hook to the head. Both hooks need to be in quick succession without a pause.

▼ Punch Flurries

Feint Jab - Straight Right – Left Hook – Straight Right

With your left fist, appear to throw the left jab, hold back, and then launch your right hand to the head instead. Next throw a left hook to the head and finish with a straight right to the head. As mentioned earlier feints are designed to fool your opponent. Feints make it appear that you are going to throw one punch, but you throw a different punch. They need to be quick, subtle, and realistic. Incorporate feints into your other punch combinations.

Punch Flurries

Flurries are light, crisp, fast, punches thrown in bunches. Throw four to six rapid-fire punches at a time. The delivery is fast so there is no time to load up on your punches. Just let your hands go.

Find a consistent punching pace

Your Virtual Opponent

Imagine you are facing an elusive opponent who is constantly moving while throwing punches at you. When facing this type of opponent, you must move continuously while throwing your punch combinations. Throw plenty of jabs to set up your power punches. For variety visualize an opponent who likes to attack and apply pressure. You will need to slip, duck, and throw counter-punches in this defensive round. Create your own battle scenarios and unleash your power and strength on the heavy bag.

KEYS TO SUCCESS

Move around and incorporate the natural swinging motion of the bag into your workout.

—

Work the bag like you are facing a real opponent.

—

Start with the basic punches and slowly build multiple punch combinations.

—

Add slipping and ducking movements while working the bag.

—

Stay on the balls of your feet. Never stand flat-footed.

HEAVY BAG DRILLS

Always warm-up before you perform any of the drills and include at least one of the drills into your Fitness Boxing workout. As you become better conditioned, add two or three of the drills at the end of your workout.

▼ Your Virtual Opponent

▼ Heavy Bag Drills

Nine-Minute Heavy Bag Workout Perform this workout for 9 minutes without stopping.

Minute One - Just moving around the bag, focusing on footwork and slipping and ducking. No punching. A preparation to fight your virtual opponent.

Minutes Two and Three - Throw only jabs on the bag, including moving up and down, slipping, and ducking.

Minutes Four and Five - Throw one-two punch combinations, maintaining your movement around the bag, and forward and backward.

Minutes Six and Seven - Throw three punch combinations. Any three punch combinations you can think of, right-left-right combination, one-two and hook to the head, etc..

Ladders – throw rapid-fire jabs

Minutes Eight and Nine – Perform punch flurries – going all out with multiple non-stop punch combinations and movement.

Heavy Bag Punch Sprint

Heavy bag punch sprints are a succession of fast punches delivered for a specific amount of time and followed by a brief rest. Punch as many times as you can for a short burst, rest, and then repeat the process again.

Face the bag straight on with both arms at an equal reach distance. Get into a position that allows your arms to be extended at impact. Maintain this distance throughout the entire drill, keeping your abdominals tight. Shift the body weight slightly forward on the balls of your feet with your knees relaxed. Hit the bag with a one-two, one-two rhythm without any pauses. Keep your breathing steady throughout the sprints.

Sprint for 15 seconds, take a 15-second rest and repeat two more times. As your conditioning improves, increase your sprinting time by 5-second increments, working up to 30-second sprints. Keep your rest intervals the same length as your sprint intervals. Since your heart rate is elevated keep moving and walking around during the rest interval. Use your watch timer or a partner to indicate the sprint times. Perform the sprint sequence three to four times.

Speed sprints – punch as fast as you can

Dirty 30s – box and move

SAMPLE BEGINNER SPEED SPRINT:
Sprint 1: *15 seconds* - **Rest:** *15 seconds*
Sprint 2: *15 seconds* - **Rest:** *15 seconds*
Sprint 3: *15 seconds* - **Rest:** *15 seconds*

Sprint training challenges your upper body musculature and cardio-respiratory system for maximum fitness results. This sprint recreates the maximum punch-speed and recovery ratio that are important in boxing, providing enhanced conditioning for individual fitness and sports.

30/30/30

This very challenging three-part drill is broken down into 30-second intervals and needs to be repeated twice in a 3-minute round.

1st 30 seconds
Punch and Move
In your boxing stance, punch the heavy bag at a fast pace, moving and throwing quick combinations as you circle the bag. Mix up your punches by throwing a variety of jabs, hooks, crosses, and body shots.

2nd 30 seconds
High Knee Run and Punching
Face the bag straight on. Punch the heavy bag non-stop with both hands while running on the spot, lifting your knees high.

Throw punches with both hands

3rd 30 seconds
Knockout!
Return to your boxing stance and hit the bag full force like you are trying to knock out your opponent. Throw as many punches as possible, using proper technique, leverage, and rotation.

Do not take a break.
Repeat the sequence again.

4th 30 seconds
Punch and Move
In your boxing stance punch the heavy bag at a fast pace, moving and throwing quick combinations as you circle the bag.

5th 30 seconds
High Knee Run and Punching
Facing the heavy bag, punch non-stop with both hands while running on the spot, lifting your knees high.

6th 30 seconds
Knockout!
Return to your boxing stance and go all out hitting the bag.

If a training partner is available they can call the 30-second intervals. If not, then you will require a timer to indicate when to move onto the next 30-second interval.

THIS IS A GREAT CARDIOVASCULAR CONDITIONING WORKOUT

Dirty 30s – knockout punches

▼ Push-Up – down position

Push-Up and Punch Drill

Start by throwing one crisp 1-2 punch combination on the heavy bag and then immediately drop down to the floor and perform one push-up. Immediately jump up into your boxing stance and perform another 1-2 combination. Repeat this sequence for 60 seconds. Maintain correct punching form, followed by properly executed push-ups. Push-ups are performed with your gloves on, keeping your wrists straight and strong. Your body weight needs to be centred through the knuckle portion of the gloves and your body held straight and strong. Breath naturally especially when performing your push-ups.

This drill focuses on the musculature of the upper body and shoulder muscles. You can modify the push-up by placing both of your knees on the floor.

These heavy bag drills can be performed on all of the larger bags; uppercut bag, aqua training bag, and uppercut and hook wall mounted bag.

▲ Push-Up – up position

Straight right

Sample Workout:

This mini-workout includes seven rounds. Make sure to rest for one-minute after each round of work.

Shadow Box – *1 x 3-minute round*
(This is a warm-up round. Focus on proper punch techniques, keeping your feet moving and focusing on your foot work. Your heart rate will increase. Perform only one round.)

Skip – *2 x 3-minute rounds*
(Jump at a challenging pace, mix up the foot work. Perform two rounds.)

Heavy Bag – *3 x 3-minute rounds*
(Start with the basic punches, add more combinations and power with each round. Perform three rounds.)

Push-Up and Punch Drill – jab

▼ Modified push-up

Shadow Box - *1 x 3-minute round*
(This is a cool down round and will lower your heart rate. Punch with little intent. Perform one round.)

Choosing a Heavy Bag
Whether you are training at home, at a fitness club, or working out at a boxing club there are numerous styles and sizes of heavy bags specific to your training requirements.

Hanging Bags
Hanging bags weigh from 23 kg (50 lb) to 110 kg (250 lb). The heavier bags move less, are less forgiving and more jarring when hit. Synthetic, vinyl-coated bags can take a pounding, however we find high quality leather bags are the most durable. The firmness of the bag will depend on both the internal packing density and the exterior material. For home use, it is worthwhile to spend a bit more money and purchase a high-quality heavy bag. Depending on your needs and experience, your weight, height, and punching strength will influence the size of the bag you purchase.

Floor bags
Floor bags can weigh up to 180 kg (400 lb). This added weight is needed to keep the bag from tipping when being punched. They are fairly portable and easily placed in an exercise area and can be purchased at most sports stores. The disadvantage of a floor bag is the absence of the swinging motion. The swinging motion of a hanging bag forces you to move with the bag and time your strikes.

Choosing a bag depends on a few variables. If you are new to hitting the heavy bag you want a softer bag, 30 kg (60 lb) to 36 kg (80 lb). If the bag is too dense, the punching impact over time can stress the muscles and joints of the hands, arms and shoulders. If you are experienced you will want to strike a more solid bag over 36 kg (80 lb) to 54 kg (120 lb).

Another consideration is your actual weight. It is often suggested that you should use a bag that is approximately half your body weight.

Body Weight

63 kg (139 lb or less)
64 kg to 72 kg (140 lb to 159 lb)
73 kg to 82 kg (160 lb to 180 + lb)

Heavy Bag

27 kg (60 lb)
36 kg (80 lb)
45 + kg (100 + lb)

Uppercut Bag

An uppercut bag is basically a heavy bag... hung horizontally. The angle of the bag allows you to execute uppercuts effectively. This is a great piece of equipment that allows you to develop this inside, close-range punch.

To effectively hit the uppercut bag, address the bag in your on-guard stance, knees slightly bent, and core muscles held tight. As you throw the uppercut, ensure the knuckle portion of your glove is flush against the underside of the bag. Practice throwing left and right uppercuts. To land a left uppercut, shift your weight slightly to the left side, with the left elbow tucked in by the side of your body and your knees bent. To land a right uppercut, shift your weight slightly to the right side, right elbow in, and knees bent. Try throwing a left and a right uppercut consecutively, bending your knees and shifting your weight from side to side. Put three uppercuts together, remembering to transfer your weight from one side to the other side. Throw a left-right-left uppercut sequence, pause, and then a right-left-right uppercut sequence, increasing your punch speed and power. Remember not to wind up or pull back your arms before throwing your uppercuts.

You can effectively work on combinations that include uppercuts, hooks, and straight punches. Use the underside of the bag for uppercuts, end of the bag for hooks, and the centre of the bag for your straight punches. Straight punches set up your short punches, so you want to practice standing far enough away from the uppercut bag to throw effective straight punches and then move in closer to land your uppercuts. Move back out before you start another combination. Add hooks to your sequences by using either end of the bag. Stand off to the right side of the bag to throw a right hook. Stand off to the left side of the bag to throw a left hook.

Basic Uppercut Combinations

Combination One: *Jab-Jab-Uppercut*
Start in your boxing stance in front of the bag, throw two quick left jabs as you move forward. Immediately follow with a short right uppercut. Repeat.

Combination Two: *1-2 – Uppercut*
Start by throwing a one-two combination, (left-jab and straight right). After your right hand has landed you should be in the correct position to throw a short, left uppercut. Quickly move away and repeat. Build onto this combination by adding a right uppercut, (1-2 - left uppercut-right uppercut).

Combination Three: *Hook-Uppercut*
Stand off to the right side of the bag and throw a right hook, followed by a left uppercut. Turn your body and pivot off your front foot as you throw the right hook and then drive off your rear foot as you launch the left uppercut. Change ends and throw a left hook followed by a right uppercut.

KEYS TO SUCCESS

Make sure your gloves land flush against the bag. Keep your elbows in by the sides of your body as you drive the punch straight up striking with the knuckle portion of your glove.

—

Bend your knees and lower your body driving the punch upward and into the bag.

—

Keep the uppercut punch fast and tight. Do not make a large arm movement by winding up to throw the punch.

THE HOOK AND UPPERCUT WALL MOUNTED BAG

The unique design of wall-mounted bags gives you the opportunity to practice punches from a variety of angles, especially hooks and uppercuts. Practice throwing punch combinations while you move in and out of position. Aim for the circular body and head target zones on the front and sides of the bag. This is a great piece of equipment to develop and perfect your short-range punches.

Basic Combinations

Combination One: *Jab to the Body-Jab to the Head-Left Hook-Short Right*
Launch a quick jab to the mid-section of the bag, followed by a jab to the head area. Finish with a hook to the left side of the bag and a short right to the front of the bag.

▲ Jab (top) and uppercut (bottom)

Combination Two: *Jab Feint-Straight Right-Left Hook-Right Uppercut*
Feint with your left jab, move forward as you throw the right lead, followed by a short, left hook, then finish with a right uppercut.

Combination Three:
1-2, Left Hook-Right Uppercut
Throw a 1-2 (left jab-straight right) to the body. Follow with a left hook to the head zone and finish with a right uppercut. Remember to bend your knees to lower your body when throwing body punches.

KEYS TO SUCCESS

Punch and get out. The wall bag is a stationary bag so you will not experience any swinging motion. Constantly move in and out of position while throwing your punches.

—

Ensure your punches land cleanly in the target zones and not on the outer edges of the bag.

AQUA TRAINING BAG

Aqua training bags are filled with H_2O. The unique teardrop shape, combined with the water-filling, and a high quality vinyl outer shell absorbs your punches and allows you to hit harder and train longer. There is a reduction on the stress placed on your joints, reducing pain. Unlike traditional heavy bags, the energy of your punch is absorbed, which translates into less movement of the bag. The unique shape of the bag allows you to throw a variety of combinations from any angle.

The bags range from 34 kg (75 lb) up to 54 kg (120 lb) and can literally take any punch combinations you throw at them. Refer to heavy bag drills.

LARGE PUNCH BAG WRAP-UP

Pounding the bags burns serious calories, challenges both the aerobic and anaerobic cardiovascular systems, and strengthens and tones your muscles. It is a great source of tension release, a genuine primal therapy. Aim to increase the number of drills you perform in your workouts, focusing on proper technique and explosive power.

REACTIVE BAGS

The smaller bags, such as the speed bag and double-end bag, require more technical skills, quick responsive movement, and finesse. More patience is required, but the payoff is worth it.

SPEED BAG

A speed bag is a small punching bag suspended below a platform (horizontal backboard) on a swivel hook, allowing for free rotational movement. It can be mounted on the wall or from a stand.

The exterior is made of leather and this is filled with an air bladder. A variety of sizes are available with the smaller bags approximately 10 cm (8 in) length. They move fast, and rebound quickly, making them a greater challenge to hit. The largest speed bags are around 20 cm (14 in) long. They react slower and are easier to hit than the smaller bags.

The "Speed" bag is the perfect name for this timeless piece of training equipment. The bag rebounds off the backboard as fast as you hit it, forcing you to keep pace and an accurate rhythm.

Fitness Benefits

Speed bag training develops the upper body and shoulder musculature, and perfects eye-hand coordination. This training works on your timing, speed, and accuracy. It also places a demand on your cardiovascular system and improves your endurance.

The speed bag develops lightning fast reaction time which can easily translate to all sports. In any sport you are active in, such as hockey, baseball, soccer, rugby, football, volleyball, and racquet sports, (tennis and squash), speed bag training will improve your overall performance.

Reactive bag

▼ Speed Bag adjustment

Adjusting the Speed Bag

The bottom of the speed bag should be eye level if you are using a small speed bag. For a larger speed bag, the bag should be one to two inches above your chin. Some speed bag platforms are adjustable so the bag can be moved to the appropriate level for you.

The bag needs to be firm, but not rock hard. If you are having difficulty hitting the bag, let some of the air out of the bladder and it will slow down the bag movement allowing you more control.

Hitting the Speed Bag
Triplet Rhythm

The rhythm of hitting the speed bag is called a 'triplet' rhythm as the bag rebounds three times, forward-backward-forward, with each strike. So the sequence is 'strike 1-2-3'. With the first strike, the bag moves away and hits the back portion of the platform (1). It then rebounds and hits the front portion of the platform (2). The bag rebounds away once again to hit the back portion of the platform (3). This is the precise moment you strike the bag once again.

THE RHYTHM OF HITTING THE SPEED BAG IS CALLED A 'TRIPLET' RHYTHM AS THE BAG REBOUNDS THREE TIMES, FORWARD-BACKWARD-FORWARD, WITH EACH STRIKE

First strike – bag hits back of platform

Bag rebounds

Ready to strike the bag again

Proper Form

Step 1 Stand facing square to the bag with both shoulders equal distance from the bag. You do not have to be in the boxer's stance. Bring both fists up in front of your face, your arms bent and the elbows bent at about ninety degrees and tucked in by the sides of your body. Your fists are approximately 15 - 20 cm (6 - 8 in) away from the bag.

Step 2 Strike the bag in the centre making sure your knuckles land flush against the leather. Hit straight through the bag. Ensure you are not 'chopping' at the bag with your strikes. Instead visualize hitting through the bag. Once you strike the bag, immediately circle your fist back to the starting position.

Step 3 Repeat striking the bag with the 'strike-1-2-3' rhythm remembering to keep both hands up by your face. It is often the transition from striking with one hand to the other that breaks your rhythm and causes ineffective hits. Start with six to eight strikes with one hand until you become competent. Switch to the other hand. Everyone has a dominant hand, so stick with it until both hands are performing equally. Reduce the number of repetitions to four hits, down to two, and then singles.

Step 4 Single strikes. As you make contact with the bag with one hand the opposite hand immediately comes up ready to strike the bag. Repeat, keeping this semi-circular movement concise and fast. As your punch speed increases, the circular range of motion your arm goes through will become shorter. The single strike is more challenging, as the faster pace requires you to react sooner.

Focus your strikes

Focus Your Strikes

The area where your knuckles make contact on the bag and how hard you strike it will affect your ability to keep the bag under control. If you make contact with the bag too soon a clumsy and awkward rhythm will result. If you strike the bag too late, your fist will hit the underside of the bag. When starting out use medium force until you have mastered the punching rhythm.

Listen to the Rhythm

As you make faster contact with the bag it is more difficult to see the rebounds, but you will still be able to hear the sounds. The triplet sequence has a distinct sound and paying attention to these sounds will assist you in developing a smooth punching rhythm. The first sound is the bag hitting the back of the platform after you strike it. The second sound is the bag moving forward and hitting the front of the platform. The third sound is the rebound of the bag moving away from you and hitting the back of the platform once again.

As you become more proficient, increase your punch speed. Wearing hand wraps provides sufficient protection for your knuckles when striking the speed bag, however if you want more protection for your hands use speed bag striking mitts or glove wraps. The mitts have a flat punching surface and are lightly padded for extra protection. The design of the glove wraps are a combination of mesh, neoprene, and a shock absorbing gel over the knuckle region, providing extra comfort and protection.

▼ Open Hand method

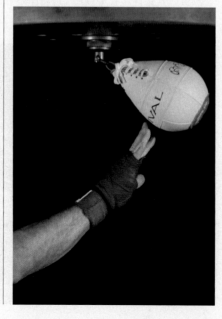

Open Hand Method

If you have difficulty controlling the speed bag, use the open-hand striking method to improve your technique. Address the bag straight-on so both hands have an equal reach to the speed bag. Keep your hands open, your palms facing the bag and drive the centre of the bag forward with your open hand. Spreading the fingers wide apart allows for more contact time with the bag and better control. Allow the bag to roll off of your fingers in a straight swinging motion. Follow through bringing your hands straight back. This open handed method will help slow down the pace of the movement of the bag for beginners until you become more efficient with the "strike-1-2-3" rhythm. Follow the steps, one through five, with open hands.

Speed Bag Combinations

Four Strikes

Four strikes with each hand allows you to get a rhythm established before you switch to the other hand. A great way to start!

Double Strikes

Reducing down to double strikes means you are bringing your other hand into play sooner.

Single Strikes

Strike alternating hands. The transition from your right fist to your left fist is quick and needs to be smooth.

Strikes with Movement

Alternate strikes with each hand, while circling the platform. Try to keep the bag steady as you are moving.

Free-Style

Effortlessly go from multiple strikes to single strikes varying your speed and rhythm. This can include short bursts of rapid fire punching for 15 to 20 seconds and then back to a regular pace. Mix it up.

KEYS TO SUCCESS

Assume the standard speed bag stance, with your feet about shoulder width apart. Have your body facing the bag straight on to ensure that both arms have equal reach.

—

Strike the bag moving your arms in small circles.

—

Bring your fists back up to striking level after hitting the bag. (Keeping your hands low will throw your timing off.)

—

Hit the bag lightly to maintain control.

—

Make contact with the belly of the speed bag, not too high, nor too low.

Use a smaller speed bag to challenge and improve your agility and eye-hand coordination. Vary the speed of the punches, slower punches interspersed with sprints. Once you have your rhythm down, move around the bag while punching.

THE DOUBLE-END STRIKING BAG

When you strike the double-end bag, it rebounds backward and forward in a random manner. The rebounding action of the double-end striking bag simulates the movement of an actual opponent. This improves reaction time and forces you to quickly make small adjustments on your punch execution and defensive moves.

Sometimes referred to as floor-to-ceiling balls, double-end bags are round, lightweight, inflatable sacks made of leather that are suspended vertically by a bungee or shock chord from the ceiling and anchored to the floor. They come in various sizes with the smaller bags being the most challenging to hit. How quickly the bag rebounds and how far it swings is also influenced by the tension of the shock chords.

Working on the double-end bag improves the speed and accuracy of your punch combinations. It also gives you an opportunity to work on defensive techniques such as slipping movements. The intention behind this reactive piece of equipment is to challenge your coordination, timing, and agility. Save your heavy hitting power for the heavy bag.

Training on the double-end bag is great for improving reaction time for many sports, like tennis and volleyball. The muscles of the shoulders, upper back, and core are recruited in order to strike the bag and must respond quickly.

It is best to wear bag gloves when hitting the double-end bag. Gloves give you more control because of the larger contact surface and they also protect your hands. When you strike the double-end bag it will move quickly away, then rebound back at you. Keep your hands in the on-guard position and your gloves held firmly in front of your head. This will prevent the bag from making contact with your face. Either counter with a punch or slip out of the way.

Keep your hands on guard

THE REBOUNDING ACTION OF THE DOUBLE-END STRIKING BAG SIMULATES THE MOVEMENT OF AN ACTUAL OPPONENT

Simulate the illusive movement of an opponent

Stay focused, ready to move

Aim for the centre of the bag

Starting Out

Start in the orthodox boxing stance, hands up, and more than a jabs length away from the bag. Ensure you are far enough away from the bag so the bag will not rebound and hit you. It is from this position you want to execute some jabs. Study how the bag rebounds back at you, at what angle, and the speed it travels. It may seem as though the bag has a mind of its own.

Aim for the centre of the bag. If the bag is spiralling off to one side, you are not catching it dead centre. The movement of the bag should be forward and

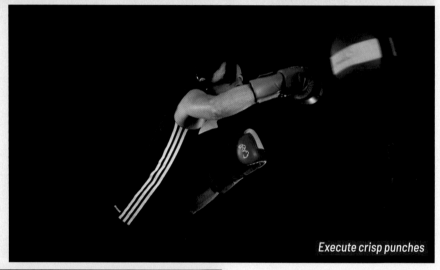
Execute crisp punches

Maintain eye contact with the bag when slipping

AIM FOR THE CENTRE OF THE BAG. IF THE BAG IS SPIRALLING OFF TO ONE SIDE, YOU ARE NOT CATCHING IT DEAD CENTRE

backward without any side-to-side motion when you strike it. Initially develop a sense of timing and discover how the bag reacts to your single straight punches, (a left jab and a straight right), before moving onto combinations.

Develop creative combinations

Basic Punch Combinations

Double and Triple Jabs
Throw two or three quick jabs. The second and third jab catches the bag on the rebound. Reset and then repeat throwing multiple jabs. Throw light and fast.

One-Two Combo
Throw a quick one-two, left jab-straight right. As your jab makes impact quickly throw your straight right before the bag fully rebounds. Throwing a one-two combination is more difficult because you must react faster. Work on developing a smooth transition from the left to the right hand always aiming for the centre of the bag.

Jab and Slip
Snap a left jab. As the bag starts to rebound quickly slip to the right, and then move back into position ready to throw your next punch. This drill simulates an incoming jab. When slipping, keep your hands up, elbows in, and eyes on the bag. Ensure your core muscles are held tight and you shift your body weight over to the right side. Repeat practicing the jab and slip until you develop your rhythm.

One-Two- Slip
Launch a quick one-two combination. Just as your straight right makes contact with the bag, slip to the left. The rebound of the bag simulates an opponent's straight right coming at you. Keep your eyes on the bag and move out of the way. Return to the on-guard position to throw another one-two.

One-Two-One-Two
Move up to a four-punch combination. Left-right-left-right. Hit the bag in the same spot with each punch, ensuring you are not pausing between the punches. Try to strike with consistency to keep the bag under control. Stay on balance. Quickly land your four punches, reset, and repeat. Repeat this rapid-fire sequence for 60 seconds.

▼ Sprints

one piece of equipment that imitates sparring against a live opponent. The constant movement of the bag simulates an opponent moving and changing direction, and the rebound action replicates oncoming punches. Master your footwork, directional changes, and rapid-fire punches developing creative combinations and defensive moves.

KEYS TO SUCCESS

Keep your fists up by your chin, elbows close to your body and eyes on the target.

—

Focus on striking the bag flush and dead centre.

—

Throwing hard, wild punches on the double-end bag will cause it to move erratically. Instead strike the bag with light, crisp, punches. This will enable you to develop a smooth punch rhythm.

—

Save the power and strength for the heavy bag.

—

When slipping, practice moving your head and shoulders just enough to avoid the rebound of the bag. If the slips are over-exaggerated, it will throw you off-balance and put you out of position to counterpunch effectively.

—

Maintain a balanced stance staying on the balls of your feet.

Left-Left-Right/Right-Right-Left
This six-punch combination requires you to focus on light, fast, punches emphasizing technique, not power. Throw two quick strikes with your left hand and follow with a short right. Immediately throw two quick rights followed by a left jab. Complete the six-punch combination, take a slight pause, and repeat. If you are having difficulty with this combination, break it into two parts. Practice the first part of the sequence, left-left-right, over and over until you have the bag under control. Then work on the second half, right-right-left. Finally put the full six-punch sequence together. Repeat for one to two minutes.

Double-end Bag Speed Sprint
Facing the bag square on, strike the bag with the right then left hand with rapid fire, non-stop punching. Focus to land your strikes dead centre on the bag and throw as fast as you can to keep the bag moving.

Freestyle on the Double-End Bag
In order to develop your timing and rhythm, dedicate several rounds working on the double-end bag during your boxing workout. Remember this is the

Freestyle on the double-end bag

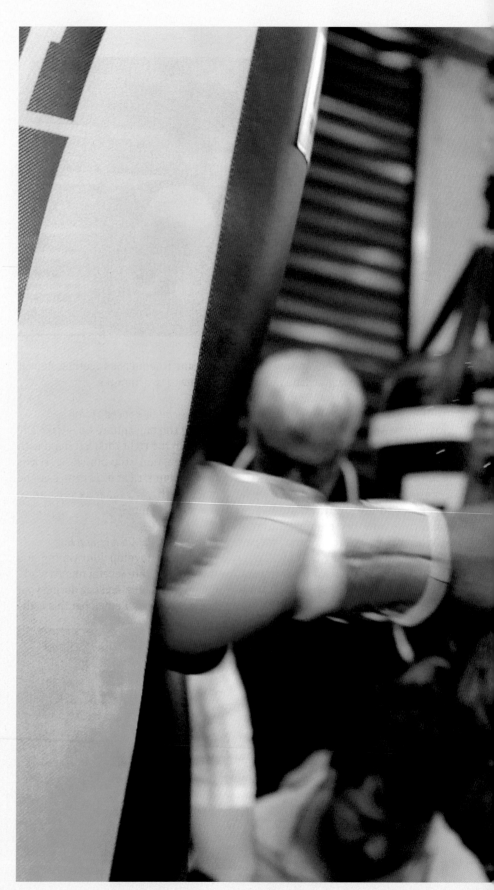

The unique qualities of the various large punching bags and reactive bags challenge your fitness capabilities, your mental focus, and develop your skill levels and your physicality.

Always execute your punches and movement utilizing proper technique. If you make this commitment to challenge yourself, improvements in timing, eye-hand coordination, quick reflexes, agility, speed, and power will be achieved. Improvements in your cardiovascular fitness, upper and lower body muscular strength, definition, and endurance, core strength, and balance will all be enhanced.

The quick reflexes and fast movements that result from training on the large bags and reactive bags provide a dynamic training experience unlike any other workout.

Floyd Mayweather Jr.

PUNCH MITT WORKOUTS

▼ Punch Mitt Training

Punch mitts develop power, speed, and accuracy

Punch mitts require complete mental focus and coordination

PUNCH MITT FUNDAMENTALS

PUNCH MITT TRAINING CAN BE AN INCREDIBLY DYNAMIC, FUN, AND CHALLENGING WORKOUT EXPERIENCE. IT IS THE CLOSEST THING TO REPLICATING A SPARRING SESSION. IT DEVELOPS PRECISE SYNCHRONIZATION OF POWER, SPEED, AND ACCURACY.

Punch mitts, also known as target mitts, focus mitts, and punching pads are hand-held padded mitts made from dense foam covered by leather or vinyl. The mitts are held by a training partner or by a coach. The catcher (coach) and the puncher work together to create an exhilarating workout, that is always engaging. The catcher gives clear and concise directions to the puncher and the puncher responds quickly and skilfully. If an experienced coach is not available, choose a training partner with a similar skill level. Working together as a team is the key when training on punch mitts and learning both roles is essential.

Punch mitt training is a blank canvas allowing you to create an engaging, responsive workout experience. You get to work on offense and defence simultaneously. It requires complete mental focus and coordination. There are many unique advantages of mitt-training. You receive instantaneous feedback from the catcher. Since you are continuously moving around a live partner, your reactive skills are challenged, and improvements are assured.

THE CATCHER

The catcher sets the pace by giving instructions to their partner and must be comfortable controlling the action. Basic number sequences can be assigned for specific punches and combinations. The catcher must clearly and concisely call out punch combinations and be ready to receive the punches. The catcher calls out a number, and the puncher throws the appropriate punch. Controlling what punch is coming allows the catcher to angle the mitt

▼ The Catcher

properly and anticipate the force of the punch. The catcher counterbalances the force of the incoming punch by 'feeding' the mitt into each blow.

Catcher Basics

When working mitts with a partner your arm position is similar to the on-guard boxing stance, with the palms turned toward your partner ready to receive a punch. Keep your elbows slightly bent to absorb the impact of the incoming punches. Maintain stability in the body, legs, and feet staying in the classic boxing stance. Always keep your eyes on your partner and clearly communicate the combinations to be executed.

The catcher's job is to have the mitts in the correct position to receive the punches. When catching straight punches, the mitts need to be facing forward. When catching hooks turn the palm of the mitt inward. When catching uppercuts turn the palm of the mitts downward, toward the floor. The mitts are generally held around shoulder level, but will need to be lowered slightly if training with a shorter partner or raised slightly if training with a taller partner. When two orthodox partners are working with the mitts, the left focus mitt catches the left jab and the right focus mitt catches the straight right. The same follows for hooks and uppercuts.

The catcher provides dynamic resistance by moving the punch mitts forward slightly to meet the incoming punches. This is called 'feeding' the punches and provides the proper feel, distance, and resistance for the puncher. The receiving and resisting motion helps to reduce the impact on the catcher's shoulders. Catching punches can be a workout in itself, so be prepared by warming up the arms and shoulder regions.

Don't Tune Out

Stay focused on your technique and on your partner so you can time and angle the mitts to safely catch the punches. It is important not to let your mind wander. Be mindful and encourage and challenge your partner.

Stay focused

TIPS FOR CATCHING FOR A 'SOUTHPAW'

When an orthodox catcher is working with a 'southpaw' puncher, the catcher always mimics the 'southpaw' stance with the right foot forward. The catcher stands with the right foot forward, catches the 'southpaw' right jab, with the right mitt and catches the straight left with the left mitt. The right focus mitt catches the right hooks and uppercuts, and the left focus mitt catches the left hook and uppercuts.

Generally, it is easiest to catch for someone who has the same dominant hand as you and the same boxing stance. If you are right hand dominant, lead with your left foot forward and the left mitt ready (orthodox). If you are left hand dominant, lead with the right foot forward and the right mitt ready (southpaw).

Hold the mitts in the correct position

▼ The Puncher

THE PUNCHER

Working on punch mitt drills with a partner allows you to perfect your punches while moving and responding quickly to changing circumstances. The catcher mimics the movement of an actual opponent. Unlike working on the heavy bag, the target continually moves and adjustments need to be made with your footwork, body position, and punch execution.

Puncher Basics

Start by assuming the on-guard position, ready to respond to the catcher's commands. Stand slightly more than a jab length away from the catcher and be prepared to throw the requested punches. Stay alert and be ready to move in and out as you throw your punches. Remain on-balance, and light on your feet while throwing your punches with proper technique, accuracy, and speed.

Working Together

The catcher selects the combinations and sets the pace of each round. It is crucial for the puncher to pay attention to all instructions from the catcher. Both must focus on the task, working together to create a safe training environment and developing smooth transitions between combinations. Work hard and always give your best effort.

All of our combinations are based on the puncher starting in the classic boxing stance with the left foot forward. Left jabs are thrown to the catcher's left focus mitt and the straight right punches are thrown to the catcher's right focus mitt. Left hooks are thrown to the catcher's left focus mitt. Right uppercuts are thrown to the catcher's right focus mitt.

Catcher must clearly communicate

Call and Catch Method

The catcher "calls" out specific punches and combinations. The puncher responds. This style of punch mitt training allows for improvements in punching technique and building basic and more advanced combinations.

▼ The Puncher Basics

BASIC DRILLS

Building Combinations

Clear communication between the catcher and the puncher is essential. Both the catcher and puncher must keep each other in view at all times. The catcher is the lead person with the puncher following the calls. All combinations are described with both the catcher and the puncher in the orthodox boxing stance.

Start with catching and receiving the basic single punches using the following number sequencing.

Assigning Numbers to Basic Punches

1: Left jab 2: Straight right
3: Left hook 4: Right uppercut

Catcher calls 1:
puncher executes a left jab.

—

Catcher calls 2:
puncher executes a straight right.

—

Catcher calls 1-2:
puncher executes a left jab-straight right combination.

—

Catcher calls 1-2-3:
puncher executes a left jab-straight right-left hook combination.

—

Catcher calls 1-2-3-4:
puncher executes a left jab-straight right-left hook-right uppercut combination.

When starting to train with punch mitts, the catcher and the puncher need to practice throwing and catching the basic punches repeatedly to develop technique, reaction time, and fluidity. Entire rounds devoted to throwing jabs and one-two's while moving around is a good way to start. It allows the puncher and catcher to become familiar with the timing of the punches and the distances required to execute effective punches.

'Punch and Get Out' Drill

Boxers are continually shifting between offensive and defensive manoeuvres, looking for opportunities to set up an attack and then quickly move away to a safe distance. The 'punch and get out' drill focuses on using your legs to move into proper range to deliver punches and immediately moving out of range. This three-minute drill is broken down into a 30-second interval starting with single punch executions and gradually building a complete combination.

Three-Minute Round Breakdown

Jab (30 seconds):
For the first 30 seconds the puncher focuses on only throwing crisp, left jabs. With the hands held high in the on-guard position move forward delivering a crisp, left jab to the catcher's left punch mitt. Quickly step out and return to the on-guard position. Vary the time you spend moving around before throwing the next jab. The emphasis for the puncher is to find proper punch range, to become comfortable with balanced footwork, and to maintain a good pace. The role of the catcher for this drill is to feed the punch mitt at the correct angle and to provide some resistance. The catcher allows the puncher to set the punching pace and to move around freely.

Straight Right *(30 seconds):*
For the next 30-second interval the puncher throws only straight rights, concentrating on moving in, landing the punch, moving out, and getting ready to set up the next punch. Launch the punch by driving off the trail foot and then quickly return to the balanced boxing

▼ Basic Drills

Left hook

Left jab

Right uppercut

Straight right

stance. Do not rush your punches. The foot movement portion of the drill is just as important as the punches. Work on moving in and out, and side-to-side to develop smooth footwork.

One-Two Combination
(30 seconds):
Move in toward the catcher, throw the one-two (left jab- straight right) combination and then move away. The catcher ensures that the puncher returns their hands up high to protect their face after each combination. Focus on smooth transitions from one punch to the next. The catcher must have both mitts in a ready position to receive the quick one-two.

One-Two-Three Combination
(30 seconds):
This three-punch combination, (jab-straight right-left hook) starts with the puncher stepping forward in order to land the left jab, immediately following with a straight right, and finishing with a short, left hook. After the left hook is landed step away immediately and move around. Repeat the sequence. The catcher must have the mitts ready at the proper angle to receive the punches. The puncher focuses on executing crisp punches and moving smoothly.

One-Two-Three-Four Combination
(30 seconds):
The puncher steps in with the left jab, followed by a straight right, then a short, left hook, and finishing up with the right uppercut, (jab- straight right-left hook-right uppercut). Begin by throwing light punches concentrating on the technical execution of each punch. Focus on smooth transitions from one punch to the other. As soon as you land the final punch in the sequence, (right uppercut), make sure your hands are in the on-guard position. Step out, reset, and repeat the sequence. The catcher must have the focus mitts in the proper position a split second before the punch makes contact with the mitt.

Four Punch Flurry
(30 seconds):
For the last 30 seconds of the round throw a quick four punch flurry, one-two, one-two (left-right, left-right), and then move out quickly. The focus is on speed, not power. Keep your punches crisp and keep your hands up.

KEYS TO SUCCESS

Ensure you are not throwing your punches with too much force as this often leads to sloppy punches and the loss of balance. Strong, efficient punches are the result of executing with proper technique.

—

After every punch sequence move out of range and get ready for your next combination.

—

When catching, feed the punches by moving the mitts slightly forward to catch the incoming punch. Keep the arms slightly bent to assist with absorption of the punch impact.

—

The main purpose of punch mitt training is to improve speed, accuracy, and provide an exhilarating workout.

—

Before moving onto the more advanced focus mitt drills ensure you are proficient with the basic combinations.

ADVANCED PUNCH MITT DRILLS

Advanced punching combinations are more complex, and slipping and ducking moves are incorporated into the drills. Intense focus is required to ensure proper execution, timing, and safety.

Defensive Moves
Skilful boxers utilize defensive moves such as slipping, ducking, blocking, and parrying punches. We will be focusing on two important defensive moves, slipping and ducking in order to add a sense of realism to your workout.

Slipping
In boxing, slipping punches is an essential defensive technique. Punch mitt training is the perfect tool to master the slipping motion since the catcher is simulating throwing a punch toward you. When executed properly, slipping moves work your leg and core muscles. Your previous training of visualising punches coming at you and slipping while shadowboxing, hitting the heavy bag, and double-end bag will prepare you for slipping when training with the punch mitts. Stay focused and react quickly when practicing slipping combinations. Always keep the hands up in the on-guard position bending at the waist and knees slightly, and shifting the body to the left or the right to avoid the punch. Do not drop your hands and do not look at the floor. Keep your eyes on your partner at all times.

When the catcher simulates throwing a straight right or left, it is executed slowly, with minimal intent, and aimed toward the puncher's shoulders and not the head region. The catcher must give the puncher sufficient time to slip out of the way.

Slipping a Left Jab: The head, body, and shoulders move as one unit to the right. Keep your body weight forward

▼ Basic Slipping Combo

Slipping a left jab

Slipping a straight right

A Puncher throws a left jab

B Puncher follows with a straight right

C Catcher simulates a left jab, puncher slips right

D Catcher simulates straight right, puncher slips to the left

and stay off your heels, as the tendency is to lean back on the trailing foot.

Slipping a Straight Right: Dip to the left, moving your head, shoulder and body together. Always return to your balanced boxing position, hands by the face, and eyes on the catcher.

Basic Slipping Combination
One–Two–Slip–Slip
The puncher starts by throwing a one-two (left jab followed by a straight right) at the catcher's mitts. The catcher immediately responds by simulating a left jab and straight right aiming for the puncher's shoulder region. These moves from the catcher should be light and controlled. To avoid the incoming left mitt, the puncher slips to the right and then immediately slips to the left to avoid the catchers incoming right and left punch mitts. Develop a smooth rhythm moving side-to-side with your hands held high, while holding your body core muscle firm.

KEYS TO SUCCESS

Always keep your eyes on your partner, whether you are catching or punching.

—

Avoid over slipping. This is when the slip is over-exaggerated and you are leaning to far to the right or to the left, leaving you off-balance.

—

Keep your body weight centred through the balls of your feet. Never sit back on your heels.

—

Ensure to keep your hands up high in the on-guard position. A common mistake is to drop your hands out of position when you shift your body weight from side-to-side.

Ducking

Boxers generally use a ducking motion to move under and avoid looping punches such as hooks.

Quickly bend the knees lowering the head and dropping the body so the punch mitt goes over the top of your head. Ducking is similar to a squat movement, bending your knees and getting down low.

When the catcher simulates a left hook, the puncher dips down under the hook and over to the right to avoid the punch. When the catcher simulates a right hook, the puncher dips down and over to the left to avoid the punch. Keep your eyes on your partner. Do not bend the body forward to avoid the punch, just bend your legs. Always return to your on-guard position quickly.

To start, the catcher throws hooks slowly and high enough for the puncher to duck under. As the puncher becomes more proficient, the catcher can increase the speed of the hooks and the lower the level of the hook.

Basic Ducking Combination

One-Two–Duck-Straight Right

The puncher launches a one-two combination at the punch mitts. The catcher returns with a simulated left hook. To avoid the hook, the puncher bends both legs and ducks under the left hook, moving to the left and then follows up by throwing a straight right. The puncher must always stay focused when manoeuvring under the punch mitt. The catcher needs to simulate the hook in a controlled manner allowing the puncher to duck underneath. As the timing of the punches and the ducking becomes accurate increase the tempo of this drill.

A

Puncher throws a left jab

B

Puncher throws straight right

▼ Ducking

Catcher simulates a left hook and puncher starts to duck

Puncher throws a left jab

Puncher throws a straight right

KEYS TO SUCCESS

Always keep your eyes on your partner before, during, and after any combination.

—

Focus on bending the legs to lower the body. Bending forward at the waist puts you off balance, increases strain on the lower back, and prohibits eye contact.

—

Bend your knees just enough to manoeuvre under the punch mitt.

—

Practice the ducking motion while you are shadowboxing in front of a mirror.

▼ Combination One (A-B-C)

BUILDING COMBINATIONS

The following six combinations and drills are broken down into easy to follow steps. Incorporate these combinations into your workout. Remember to continually communicate with your partner while throwing and catching.

Combination One: *Jab-Jab-Right*

Step 1
The puncher moves forward while executing a left jab. (A)

—

Step 2
Continue stepping forward as the second jab is launched. (B)

—

Step 3
Follow with a straight right from a balanced position. (C)

(The catcher must synchronize their movement with the puncher. In this case the catcher moves backward with each punch.)

Throw a quick jab

▼ Combination One (A-B-C)

Immediately follow with another quick jab

Finish with a straight right

▼ Combination Two (A-B-C-D-E)

Start by throwing a right upper cut

Follow with a left uppercut

Throw another right uppercut

Combination Two:
Uppercut-Uppercut-Uppercut,
Left Hook-Right Cross

Step 1
Catcher holds the mitts in position to receive three uppercuts. (A-B-C)

—

Step 2
Puncher starts with the right uppercut first, then left, then right. (A-B-C)

—

Step 3
Puncher follows with a left hook and finishes with a straight right. (D-E)

Throw a short left hook

Finish the combo with a straight right

Combination Three:
Jab, Slip, Right Cross-Left Hook

Step 1
Puncher throws a left jab to the catcher's left mitt. (A)

—

Step 2
The catcher immediately comes back with a left jab, tapping the puncher on the left shoulder. (B)

—

Step 3
The puncher quickly slips to the right, pivots back with a right cross and finishes off with a left hook. Be ready to move quickly. (C-D)

Puncher comes back with a right cross

Puncher throws a left jab

Catcher simulates a left jab, puncher slips to the right

Puncher finishes with a left hook

A Puncher throws a jab

B Follows with a straight right

C Catcher simulates a left jab and puncher slips

D Puncher counters with a right

Combination Four:
*One-Two-Slip,
Right-Left-Right*

Step 1
Puncher starts this
drill with a quick one-two
combination. (A-B)

—

Step 2
Catcher simulates a
left jab as the puncher
slips to the right to avoid
the incoming jab. (C)

—

Step 3
Puncher counters with
three straight punches:
right-left-right. (D-E-F)

REMEMBER TO KEEP YOUR HANDS UP WHEN SLIPPING

E Follows with a left jab

F Finishes the combo with a straight right

Start by throwing a fast jab

Combination Five:
One-Two-One-Two, Slip-Slip, Left Hook- Straight Right

Step 1
Puncher throws four straight punches: left-right-left-right.
(A-B-C-D)

—

Step 2
Puncher slips the catcher's left and right mitt. (E-F)

—

Step 3
Puncher finishes with a left hook and a straight right. (G-H)

Follow with a straight right

Throw another jab

Follow with a straight right

Catcher simulates a left jab and puncher slips to the right

WHEN SIMULATING THE LEFT AND RIGHT PUNCH, THE CATCHER TAPS THE PUNCHER'S LEFT AND RIGHT SHOULDER

Catcher simulates a straight right and puncher slips to the left

Puncher counters with a left hook

Finish the combination with a straight right

Combination Six:
1-2-3, Duck, Left Hook-Straight Right

Step 1
Puncher starts by throwing a three-punch combination, left jab, straight right, and left hook. (A–B–C)

—

Step 2
The catcher simulates a right hook over their partner's head while the puncher ducks under the hook. (D–E)

—

Step 3
The puncher returns with a left hook and a straight right at the mitts. (F–G)

A *Start with a sharp left jab*

B *Follow with a straight right*

C *Throw a short left hook*

D *Catcher simulates a right hook, puncher ducks under*

E *Keep your eyes on your partner as you duck under*

F *Puncher returns to full height and throws a left hook*

G *Finish the combo with a straight right*

STAY FOCUSED WHEN DUCKING, BODY WEIGHT FORWARD, AND ON THE BALLS OF YOUR FEET

Start by practicing all of the combinations slowly and then gradually increase the pace. If you are having difficulty with any of the multiple punch sequences go back to basics combinations. Focus on crisp punches, proper technique, and balanced movement.

▼ Free-Style Punch Mitts

PUNCH MITT TRAINING CREATES A DYNAMIC TRAINING ENVIRONMENT THAT SHARPEN SKILLS, REFLEXES, AND DEVELOPS CORE AND UPPER BODY STRENGTH

▼ Punch and Push-Up Drill

Puncher throws a left jab

Puncher follows with a straight right

Puncher performs push-ups

Push-Ups are performed on the knuckle portion of the gloves

Free-Style Punch Mitts

Punch mitt training creates a dynamic training environment that sharpens skills, reflexes, and develops core and upper body strength. When creating your own punch combinations, it should be both challenging and fun. Work the basic combinations until you become confident with them and then add more movement and increase your punch speed. After you have perfected your skills by working on mitt drills in this chapter, start to create your own combinations. When developing your own combinations ensure they follow a logical sequence with one punch effectively setting up the next punch or movement.

Intensity

Punch mitt workouts should be modified to each individual's ability and skill level. This is accomplished by adapting the intensity level and the punch sequencing of the drills. The catcher sets the pace by allowing more or less time between punches and movement.

PUNCH MITT DRILLS

The following drills will develop your conditioning. Select one of the drills to finish your punch mitt workout. In *Chapter 10 - B.I.T.S. – Boxing Interval Training System*, a description of how to put together a complete fitness boxing training routine will be explained.

Punch and Push-Up Drill

The puncher throws the one-two combinations at the catcher's mitts and immediately drops into a push-up position and performs the same number of push-ups. Throw the left jab-straight right combination with precision each time, pausing to reset before the next combinations. It is not a sprint.

For example, the puncher starts in a boxing stance and throws the one-two combination eight times and then immediately drops to the floor and performs eight push-ups. The puncher jumps up and throws seven one-two and then performs seven push-ups,

103

then six one-two punches and six push-ups and so on. Continue going down the ladder until you throw a final one-two punch combination and one push-up. (The number of punches and push-ups are reduced by one each sequence.)

For this drill, the push-ups are performed with boxing gloves on. Place the knuckle portion of the glove on the floor and hold the wrists straight and steady. Both the gloves and your wraps will give additional support to your wrists. Keep the elbows close to the sides of the body, while lowering toward the floor. With more advanced push-ups keep the body long and legs straight. Beginners, start with a modified push-up with your knees on the floor. (Refer to Chapter Three for the description of the modified push-up.) Continue to concentrate on throwing strong, straight punches at the focus mitts.

Moving quickly from a punching position down to the push-up position and then back up to the punching position, develops overall agility and challenges your upper body muscles.

Depending on your fitness level, you may want to start at a lower number of one-twos and push-ups to start your ladder. Select the appropriate starting point for you.

Basic: Start with six 1-2's and six push-ups for a total 21 push-ups/21 punches.

Intermediate: Start with eight one-twos and eight push-ups for a total 36 push-ups/36 punches.

Advanced: Start with ten one-twos and ten push-ups for a total 55 push-ups/55 punches.

Punch Mitt Sprints

Punch mitts sprints are a rapid-fire series of straight punches, hooks, and uppercuts, followed by slipping moves. The purpose of punch mitt sprints is to challenge and improve your endurance. This is a high energy drill focusing on both speed and accuracy.

Puncher

The puncher starts this drill by facing the catcher straight on and not in the traditional boxing stance. Keeping the hands in the on-guard position, and the body weight slightly forward, punch as quickly as possible. Always maintain proper punch technique. Punch non-stop, starting with the straight punches for the specified amount of time, move directly into throwing hooks for the specified time, and then following with uppercuts. The puncher throws straight punches, hooks, and uppercuts without a break. Then with your hands up, slip from side to side. Slips provide a brief punching break, keeps your heart rate elevated, and works your core muscles with the side-to-side movement.

Repeat the punching sprint, throwing left and right straight punches, left and right hooks, and left and right uppercuts. To add variety, you can add ducking movements instead of slips at the end. When the ducking move is performed the core and leg muscles are targeted.

Even though this is a conditioning drill and you want to maintain a swift pace, it is imperative that you execute the punches with proper technique. Extend your arms for the straight punches, rotate through the body when throwing hooks, and roll your shoulders with your elbows tucked in when throwing uppercuts.

Catcher

The catcher also faces the punching partner straight on, holding the punch mitts at the correct angle to receive the flurry of punches. To receive the straight punches, the mitts are held facing the puncher, for hooks the mitts are held with the palms facing inward, and for uppercuts the mitts are held with the palms facing downward.

For this drill, the catcher may also assist the puncher in working on slipping. At the end of the first punch sequence the catcher simulates left and right punches. The catcher throws straight lefts and rights at a consistent non-stop pace aiming at the puncher's shoulders. The puncher slips side to side.

▼ Punch Mitt Sprints

Start by throwing rapid fire straight lefts and rights

Immediately follow with left and right hooks

SAMPLE SPRINT INTERVAL:
Sprint One
Straight lefts and rights	*20 seconds*
Left and right hooks	*20 seconds*
Left and right uppercuts	*20 seconds*
Slipping side-to-side	*20 seconds*

Sprint Two
Straight lefts and rights	*20 seconds*
Left and right hooks	*20 seconds*
Left and right uppercuts	*20 seconds*
Slipping side-to-side	*20 seconds*

After you have gone through the sprint sequence twice, you may want to switch roles with your training partner. Work at intervals of 20 seconds. As your fitness level improves increase the sprint time to a 30 to 40-second interval.

PUNCH MITTS SPRINTS ARE A RAPID-FIRE SERIES OF STRAIGHT PUNCHES, HOOKS, AND UPPERCUTS, FOLLOWED BY SLIPPING MOVES

CORE STRENGTH TRAINING

Punch Mitt Sit-Ups
This two-minute partner drill challenges your core muscles. The puncher, wearing gloves, starts by lying down with the knees bent and feet on the ground. A full sit-up is performed and at the top of the sit-up four quick punches are thrown to the catcher's mitts. The puncher returns back to the ground and repeats the sequence of sitting up and throwing four more quick punches.

Four straight right and left punches are thrown at the top of each sit-up. Repeat for 20 seconds. Next throw four left and right hooks at the top of each sit-up. Repeat for 20 seconds and finally throw four left and right uppercuts at the top of each sit-up and repeat for 20 seconds. The sit-ups and punches are continuous. This will take one minute.

Next, throw left and right uppercuts as fast as possible

Catcher simulates throwing lefts and rights, puncher slips side to side

Puncher keeps hands in on-guard position and eyes always on training partner

▼ Punch Mitt Sprints

Start in sit-up position

Puncher delivers four straight punches after each sit-up

Immediately repeat the above sit-up exercise cycle for another minute. The catcher must hold the mitts at the proper angle to receive each series of punches. The punches should be light with emphasis on performing smooth sit-ups each time. Find a comfortable pace and breathe naturally for this two-minute drill.

SAMPLE:

Sit-up - throw four straight left and right punches –lie back. Repeat sequence for 20 seconds.

Sit-up - throw four left and right hooks –lie back. Repeat sequence for 20 seconds.

Sit-up - throw four left and right uppercuts –lie back. Repeat sequence for 20 seconds.

PUNCH MITT WORKOUTS

Three punch mitt workouts are described as follows. Choose the appropriate workout level. With the catcher and puncher working together, the workouts follow the boxing pattern of a three- minute workout and a one-minute rest in between each round.

To add variety to the three-minute combination drills, have the puncher throw only jabs, moving around, and working on foot work, and then return to the drill. As you become more proficient at the workouts, choose the combinations you want to improve upon.

▼ Punch Mitt Workouts

Basic Mitt Workout (6 rounds)
Start with a round of shadowboxing to warm -up. Use this three-minute round to increase your heart rate and increase oxygen circulation. Remember to take a one-minute rest in between each round. The first round on the mitts

Puncher throws four left and right hooks after each sit-up

Puncher throws four left and right uppercuts after each sit-up

is the Punch and Get Out Drill. This is a great drill to start your punch mitt workout, beginning with single punches and gradually building combinations. In the next round, practice the basic slipping combination, then combination one, then combination two. Finally, cool-down with a shadow box round, punching lightly and moving around.

SUMMARY
Round 1 - *Shadow Box - warm-up*
Round 2 - *Punch and Get Out Drill*
Round 3 - *Basic Slipping Combination - One–Two–Slip-Slip*
Round 4 - *Combination One: Jab-Jab-Right*
Round 5 - *Combination Two: Uppercut-Uppercut- Uppercut, Left Hook-Right Cross*
Round 6 - *Shadow Box - cool-down*

Intermediate Mitt Workout (8 rounds)
This 8-round workout starts with one easy warm-up round of shadow-boxing, followed by a more intense round of shadowboxing. For this second round of shadowboxing, throw a greater variety of punches with active footwork. Incorporate slipping and ducking moves. For the third round, perform The Punch and Get

Out Drill throwing single punches and gradually building combinations. In round 4, add ducking by completing the Basic Ducking Combination, (One–Two–Duck–Straight Right), for 3 minutes. Continue with combination three, then four, and finally, punch mitt sprints. For round 8, throw easy punches in the shadowboxing round in order to cool down.

SUMMARY
Round 1 - *Shadow Box - warm-up*
Round 2 - *Shadow Box (add more intensity and punch variety)*
Round 3 - *Punch and Get Out Drill*
Round 4 - *Basic Ducking Combination - One-Two–Duck-Straight Right*
Round 5 - *Combination Three: Jab, Slip, Right Cross-Left Hook*
Round 6 - *Combination Four: One-Two-Slip, Right-Left-Right*
Round 7 - *Punch Mitt Sprints*
Round 8 - *Shadow Box - cool-down*

Advanced Mitt Workout (10 rounds)
The 10-round workout starts with an easy shadow-boxing round, followed by a more intense round of shadow-boxing. In the third shadowboxing round, hold light hand weight, (1-1.5 kg; 2-3 lb), while executing a variety

of punches and always concentrate on proper execution for all of the punches. Perform combinations four, five, and six for the next rounds. In round 7, Punch and Push Up Drill, focus on proper push-up body position and form. To really challenge and improve your endurance, complete round 8, Punch Mitt Sprints. Put your effort into fast quick punches that make accurate contact with the punch mitt. In round 9, shadow-box to cool down lowering your heart rate. Finish off with sit-ups and a rapid-fire series of straight punches, hooks, and uppercuts by performing Punch Mitt Sit-Ups in round 10.

SUMMARY
Round 1 - *Shadow Box - warm-up*
Round 2 - *Shadow Box (add more intensity and punch variety)*
Round 3 - *Shadow Box (hold light hand weights, 1-1.5 kg; 2-3 lb)*
Round 4 - *Combination Four: One-Two-Slip, Right-Left-Right*
Round 5 - *Combination Five: One-Two-One-Two, Slip-Slip, Left Hook-Straight Right*
Round 6 - *Combination Six: 1-2-3, Duck, Left Hook- Straight Right*
Round 7 - *Punch and Push-Up Drill*
Round 8 - *Punch Mitt Sprints*
Round 9 - *Shadow Box - cool down*
Round 10 - *Punch Mitt Sit-Ups*

When you watch great boxers and their trainers work the punch mitts, you will notice the fluid precision and rhythmic movement that results in improved endurance, muscular strength, and sharpened offensive and defensive skills. Punch mitt training is always physically challenging and mentally engaging. As you become more proficient at punch mitt training, work freestyle, improvising the punch combinations and providing a varied program. Always work at a level that is specific to each person's specific needs and skill level.

Fluid precision and rhythmic movement

RUN LIKE A BOXER

ROADWORK HAS ALWAYS BEEN A KEY ELEMENT TO A BOXER'S TRAINING. IT IS STILL A CRUCIAL PART OF THE CONDITIONING PROGRAM, BUT THE WAY THE TRAINING IS EXECUTED IS VERY DIFFERENT. TODAY, BOXERS ARE MORE CONSCIENTIOUS ABOUT DESIGNING THEIR ROADWORK TRAINING TO MIMIC THE UNIQUE DEMANDS OF THE SPORT.

Running like a boxer will help you develop an improved breathing pattern, feeling less winded and giving you more energy for your workouts. The varied running routines improves leg strength and enhances side-to-side, forward, and backward footwork.

Aerobic versus Anaerobic Training

Most coaches and trainers acknowledge that the sport of boxing is mainly an anaerobic sport with approximately 70 to 80 % anaerobic demands and 20 to 30% aerobic demands.

Aerobic means that oxygen is readily available for the working muscles over a longer period of time. Aerobic activity occurs when a boxer is moving around the ring evading an opponent, setting up an attack, and catching their breath. Running longer distances at a moderate pace will train your aerobic capabilities.

Roadwork refers to various types of running styles and there are many different ways you can incorporate it into your workout to improve your fitness level. Roadwork must include variety, such as bursts of energy interspersed with less intensity, lateral or sideways movement, and forward and backward activity.

All types of cardio-training are important for fitness. No longer is 100% of the roadwork based on long, slow runs using the aerobic conditioning approach. To fight effectively, a boxer needs to train to maintain his strength and endurance, but he also must be able to produce intermittent explosive bursts throughout every round. A weekly running program consists of intervals, sprints, and an occasional aerobic longer run. The longer runs help to maintain and improve cardio-respiratory endurance to last the length of a boxing match. Interval training develops the conditioning required to sustain a higher effort level for a specific time or distance. Sprints prepare the body for an all-out effort.

Anaerobic means to perform an activity without oxygen being readily available to the heart, lungs and working muscles. When boxing, the demands on the muscles and cardiovascular system are stressed at high intensities for short time periods and oxygen is not readily accessible. Anaerobic conditioning is necessary during a fight for the quick bursts of energy required to throw multiple punch combinations. Interval running programs including sprints and higher intensity demands will improve your anaerobic capacity.

EFFECTIVE RUNNING TIPS

Feet
Proper foot placement is important when running. Land with your foot lightly on the ground between your heel and mid-foot, then roll quickly toward the toe region. Push off the front of your foot, getting extra power from your ankle and calf muscle. Keep the contact time of the foot with the ground to a minimum. The aim is to achieve a quick turnover time.

Aim for quick foot turnover

Knees
The knee position establishes your stride length. Seasoned endurance runners lift their knees only slightly giving them a quick leg turnover and a shorter stride. This allows for an efficient forward movement that wastes very little energy. When sprinting, the knees are lifted higher in order to produce maximum leg power. The knees move straight forward as you lift them and directly below the hips as you land. When your foot strikes the ground, a slightly bent knee will absorb some of the impact.

Hips
Your hips are key to good running posture and when the torso and back are straight and upright, the hips will fall into the correct alignment. Keep the hips in a neutral position, avoiding an extreme tilt forward or backward.

Torso
Hold your torso upright with the core muscles held taut, your head up, looking forward, and your shoulders relaxed. Running in this tall position assists with optimal breathing and proper stride length.

Arms
Swing your arms straight forward and backward in combination with your leg strides. Keep your elbows at a 90 degrees angle for the most part. If you feel your arms, hands, and neck region tensing up, drop your arms to your sides and shake them out. Ensure your hands are relaxed in an unclenched fist.

Shoulders
Keep the shoulders low and relaxed throughout your run. As you become tired the tendency is to raise the shoulders up toward the ears and often dip side to side with each foot strike. Relaxed shoulders also play an important role in maintaining the proper posture for efficient running.

Keep neck and shoulders relaxed

Head Tilt
Posture is extremely important when running and assists in your running efficiency. Look straight ahead in front of you. This will help you to maintain a straight neck and back, and your chin in a neutral position. Do not look down at your feet.

HOW TO START RUNNING

Warm-up Before You Run
It is important to warm-up before you start to run. A great way to increase the blood flow in your body is to warm-up by shadowboxing, moving side-to-side, and forward and backward, throwing punches. You can also warm-up by walking for five minutes at a fairly good pace, swinging the arms and stretching out the muscles if they feel tight. *(Refer to Chapter 8)*

Warm-up by shadowboxing

Walk/Run

If you are new to running, a safe approach is to walk and run in intervals. You will build stamina to run further and faster and reduce the chance of injuries in your joints and muscles. This slow and steady method of training starts with walking for a specific time or distance, followed by jogging for a specific time or distance. When beginning a running program take 24 to 48 hours in between your training. It is during these non-training rest days that the body mends and your fitness and strength improves.

▼ Walk/run method

Start by walking

Depending on your base level of fitness, start by walking and jogging or running lightly intermittently for a total of 12 to 16 minutes. Decrease the amount of time you spend walking and increase the amount of time you spend running. Work at a moderate to hard perceived exertion rate of 6 to 8, *(refer to Chapter One)*. Your breathing rate will increase. During the walking phase, walk fast and keep the heart rate elevated, still working

▼ Walk/run method

Run

at a moderate level. The first three to four weeks are generally the most difficult for novice runners. The body and musculature are adapting to the new demands placed on it. Listen to your body and monitor your running/walking time and intensity. You do not want to get into an intense training situation where you are you are gasping for air or placing too much stress on your muscles and joints.

Cool-down After Your Run

After each workout remember to perform stretches for your thighs, calfs, hips and gluteals. Take your time and execute the stretches through the full range of motion.

KEYS TO SUCCESS

Look straight forward, keeping your neck and back straight, and your chin in a neutral position.

—

Move your arms forward and backward beside the torso with each foot strike.

—

Listen to your body and work up to running a continuous distance.

—

Do not look down at your feet.

—

Land your foot softly on the ground and let your knee and ankle absorb the impact.

—

Maintain a tall posture to assist with your breathing.

—

Stop and stretch out your muscles is they become tight during a longer run.

Improving Your Running Endurance
If you are able to run for fifteen to twenty minutes comfortably, continue to increase the distance and time spent running. Make the increases every two to three weeks aiming for a continuous running/jogging for 45 minutes to 60 minutes. Run at a moderate perceived exertion rate of 6 to 7.

Remember to stretch out the muscles and joints after these longer runs, especially the hip flexors and calf muscles. *(Refer to Chapter 8)*

▼ Walk/run method

Gradually build your stamina

Improving Your Running Speed

To improve your running performance, a balance of easy running and the more difficult, faster intervals are required. Relating back to the 'overload principle', additional stress is a requirement for improved performance. Interval running sessions provide additional stress so your fitness level can adapt and evolve, and not stay at a stagnant level. Work at a perceived exertion of 6 to 7 for the basic running and then bump up the intensity to 8 to 9 for your interval running for a specified distance or time. *(Refer to Chapter One)*

CHOOSING THE RIGHT PLAN FOR YOU

Just Starting Out

If you have not been working out for over six to eight months or are not accustomed to exercising, always consult a physician before starting any exercise program.

Workout Time Total: *30 minutes*
Start walking at a comfortable pace increasing to a brisk walk to warm-up for 10 minutes. For one minute, run easily, then walk at a moderate pace for

three minutes. This interval workout will take you 16 minutes to complete. Cool down by walking at an easy, comfortable pace for 4 minutes.

Warm-up	brisk walk	10 minutes
Interval 1	easy run	1 minute
Recovery	brisk walk	3 minutes
Interval 2	easy run	1 minute
Recovery	brisk walk	3 minutes
Interval 3	easy run	1 minute
Recovery	brisk walk	3 minutes
Interval 4	easy run	1 minute
Recovery	brisk walk	3 minutes
Cool-down	easy walk	4 minutes

Progression:
Decrease the amount of time you spend walking and increase the amount of time you spend running.

Staying in Shape

If you exercise two to three times per week such as, brisk walking, hiking, fitness classes, recreational cycling, follow the program described below.

Workout Time Total: *40 minutes*
To warm-up, perform an easy jog or brisk walk for five minutes. Then increase your pace to a moderate to fast run for 15 minutes. After the 15-minute run, perform intervals of a challenging one-minute run, followed by a two-minute brisk walk or easy run. Repeat this interval four more times for a total of five intervals. Finish off walking for 5 minutes to cool down.

Warm-up	brisk walk	5 minutes
Run	moderate pace	15 minutes
Interval 1	run	1 minute
Recovery	easy run/walk	2 minutes
Interval 2	run	1 minute
Recovery	easy run/walk	2 minutes
Interval 3	run	1 minute
Recovery	easy run/walk	2 minutes
Interval 4	run	1 minute
Recovery	easy run/walk	2 minutes
Interval 5	run	1 minute
Recovery	easy run/walk	2 minutes
Cool-down	walk	5 minutes

Progression:
For the interval session, run for one-minute and walk for one-minute, repeating eight times.

Crank It Up

If you routinely exercise most days of the week and are able to run for 30 minutes non-stop, follow the program below.

Workout Time Total: *50 minutes*
To warm-up, walk briskly or jog lightly for five minutes. Run at a moderate pace for 25 minutes. For the next 15 minutes perform intervals, running at a faster pace for one minute followed by a 30-second recovery easy run or walk. Repeat alternating the one-minute run and a 30-second recovery easy run or walk for a total of ten times. Walk at a moderate pace for five minutes to cool down.

Warm-up	easy run/walk	5 minutes
Run	moderate pace	25 minutes
Interval 1	fast run	1 minute
Recovery	easy run/walk	30 seconds
Interval 2	fast run	1 minute
Recovery	easy run/walk	30 seconds
Interval 3	fast run	1 minute
Recovery	easy run/walk	30 seconds
Interval 4	fast run	1 minute
Recovery	easy run/walk	30 seconds
Interval 5	fast run	1 minute
Recovery	easy run/walk	30 seconds
Interval 6	fast run	1 minute
Recovery	easy run/walk	30 seconds
Interval 7	fast run	1 minute
Recovery	easy run/walk	30 seconds
Interval 8	fast run	1 minute
Recovery	easy run/walk	30 seconds
Interval 9	fast run	1 minute
Recovery	easy run/walk	30 seconds
Interval 10	fast run	1 minute
Recovery	easy run/walk	30 seconds
Cool down	walk	5 minutes

Progression:
At the last 10 seconds of each minute of running, increase your running speed to a sprint.

RUN LIKE A BOXER

ON THE TRACK
Training with Sprints

Adding running sprints to your workouts helps to push you beyond a fitness plateau, thereby improves your physical conditioning level. Sprints challenge your heart strength and endurance, and muscle capabilities. To perform a sprint, an all-out effort is required for 10 to 30 seconds or running a distance of approximately 200 metres. Work at a perceived exertion of 9-10.

Interval training track sprints

Distance Sprints

A basic form of interval sprint training is to sprint the same distance repeatedly. This can be easily measured if you perform the sprints on a track. Always warm-up thoroughly before starting your workout. Start by warming up your muscles and cardio system by running at an easy pace for 400 metres, (once around the track). Now perform a sprint for 200 metres, (perceived exertion level of 9-10). Keep up this running intensity for the 200 metres distance and then run/walk back to your starting point. Use the time it takes to run/walk back to the start location to recover. When sprinting breath deep into your abdomen, pump your arms, and lift the knees high. Repeat six times and cool down with an easy run/walk.

SAMPLE SPRINT

Warm-up	easy run	400 metres
Interval 1	sprint	200 metres
Recovery	easy run	200 metres
Interval 2	sprint	200 metres
Recovery	easy run	200 metres
Interval 3	sprint	200 metres
Recovery	easy run	200 metres
Interval 4	sprint	200 metres
Recovery	easy run	200 metres
Interval 5	sprint	200 metres
Recovery	easy run	200 metres
Interval 6	sprint	200 metres
Recovery	easy run	200 metres
Cool down	easy run	400 metres

Timed Sprints

Timed sprints require you to run at a perceived exertion level of 9-10, for 30 seconds. Warm up with a 6 to 10-minute easy run. Then perform a series of 30-second sprints with a one-minute recovery. Start your sprint by steadily increasing your speed to maximum. Try to recover within one minute by walking or running lightly, and then perform another all-out 30-second sprint. Perform six 30-second sprints with a one-minute rest in between. Finish off with a 6 to 10-minute easy run/walk.

SAMPLE SPRINT

Warm-up	easy run	6-10 minutes
Interval 1	sprint	30 seconds
Recovery	run/walk	1 minute
Interval 2	sprint	30 seconds
Recovery	run/walk	1 minute
Interval 3	sprint	30 seconds
Recovery	run/walk	1 minute
Interval 4	sprint	30 seconds
Recovery	run/walk	1 minute
Interval 5	sprint	30 seconds
Recovery	run/walk	1 minute
Interval 6	sprint	30 seconds
Recovery	run/walk	1 minute
Cool down	easy run	6-10 minutes

ON THE HILLS

Hill runs are a great way to challenge your overall conditioning and work at a higher intensity level without placing excessive impact on your legs, and joints. The stride range of motion is limited, thereby reducing the risk of muscle strains and pulls. The inclined surface increases the difficulty of the run. If you are running outdoors

▼ Downhill technique

Allow your stride to open up

plan a route that includes hills. When sprinting up the hill, lean slightly into the hill, keeping your chest up. You will notice that your stride length is shorter and you will have to lift your knees higher. It is best to shift your foot plant to the balls of your feet. Keep the arms and legs working in unison, pushing forward as you approach the top. Try to run past the top and then turn around returning down the hill. Relax as you run or walk down the hill, allowing gravity to help pull you along and allowing your stride to open up. Always focus on proper running technique. Warm up by running for 6 to 10 minutes and then sprint up a hill at a perceived exertion of 9 to 10, for 30 to 60 seconds. Run or walk down the hill to recover. Repeat 6 to 8 times.

▼ Hill sprints

Challenge your overall conditioning

INTERVAL HILL SPRINTS

Warm-up	run	6-10 minutes
Interval 1	hill sprint	30-60 seconds
Recovery	run/walk	down the hill
Interval 2	hill sprint	30-60 seconds
Recovery	run/walk	down the hill
Interval 3	hill sprint	30-60 seconds
Recovery	run/walk	down the hill
Interval 4	hill sprint	30-60 seconds
Recovery	run/walk	down the hill
Interval 5	hill sprint	30-60 seconds
Recovery	run/walk	down the hill
Interval 6	hill sprint	30-60 seconds
Recovery	run/walk	down the hill
Cool down	easy run	6-10 minutes

Interval running, or sprinting sessions can be performed 2 to 3 days per week and never on consecutive days. Since these workouts are intense, your body requires adequate time to recover. It is also advisable not to perform sprint intervals on the days that you train on the bags and punch mitts.

An additional benefit of training at this very high intensity is that more energy is required and therefore more calories are burned. If one of your goals is to lose weight, then incorporate sprints into your training.

IN THE GYM

Cardio-Training Alternative

Running on a treadmill is a great alternative if you are unable to run outside due to the weather or the location. Simply walk or run in place keeping up with the motorized belt that moves under your feet. The newer models provide sufficient shock absorption, a wide variety of training programs, and storage for your personal programs.

Start with the treadmill moving slowly and place one foot on either side of the belt. Step onto the moving belt. Unless you are very new to running on the treadmill, there is no need to hold onto the handrails. Move your

▼ Cardio alternatives

Treadmills are a good cardio alternative option

arms when running on the treadmill as you would when running outside. If, however you are experiencing any balance issues, then steady yourself by lightly touching the handrails. Maintain an upright posture and look straight ahead.

Running on the treadmill burns approximately the same number of calories as running outside. There is a difference though, with running on an inclined treadmill compared to running up hills. Running up hills takes more energy and burns more calories than running on an inclined treadmill.

As well, you can choose programs that will intermittently increase and decrease the pace of the belt, so you are running faster and then slower. As with any workout program remember to cool down your heart rate by walking three-five minutes and perform cool down stretches.

Treadmills can be programmed for interval workouts

ULTIMATE BOXING RUNNING ROUTINE

This unique running routine will incorporate varied footwork, directional changes, and throwing light punches while you run.

Warm-up by shadowboxing for 3 minutes, throwing punches and moving around. This will increase your heart rate and warm-up your muscles. Start running at a moderate pace for 10 minutes. After 10 minutes continue running and add some light punch sprints. Throw these punch sprints from shoulder height, alternating left and right punches, for 30 seconds.

Go back to a moderate run without punching for one minute. Repeat this one-minute run and 30-second light punch sprints, six times in total.

Next, run for five minutes at a moderate pace, then perform 30-second interval running sprints and one-minute runs. The 30-second interval sprints are performed four times ending with a run at a moderate pace for five minutes.

In order to work and improve overall footwork, side shuffles and high knees are incorporated into the next interval work. Perform a side shuffle for 20 seconds, keeping your fists up in the on-guard position, and then run forward once again for two minutes. Next perform a side shuffle leading with the opposite foot for 20 seconds. Always be aware of your surroundings and foot placement when performing side shuffles. Repeat two more times. Replace the shuffle with high knees for 20 seconds, repeat the two-minute run and 20-second high knees.

Cool down by running at an easy pace for three minutes. (Remember to perform your cool down stretches taking the muscles through the full range of motion.)

ULTIMATE BOXING RUNNING ROUTINE SUMMARY:

Warm-up	_shadow box_	_3 minutes_
Moderate run		_10 minutes_
Light punch sprints		_30 seconds_
Run		_1 minute_
Light punch sprints		_30 seconds_
Run		_1 minute_
Light punch sprints		_30 seconds_
Run		_1 minute_
Light punch sprints		_30 seconds_
Run		_1 minute_
Light punch sprints		_30 seconds_
Run		_1 minute_
Light punch sprints		_30 seconds_
Run		_5 minutes_
Sprint		_30 seconds_
Run		_1 minute_
Sprint		_30 seconds_
Run		_1 minute_
Sprint		_30 seconds_
Run		_1 minute_
Sprint		_30 seconds_
Run		_5 minutes_
Side shuffle		_20 seconds_
Run		_2 minutes_
Side shuffle		_20 seconds_
Run		_2 minutes_
Side shuffle		_20 seconds_
Run		_2 minutes_
Side shuffle		_20 seconds_
Run		_2 minutes_
High knees		_20 seconds_
Run		_2 minutes_
High knees		_20 seconds_
Cool down	_easy run_	_3 minutes_

KEYS TO SUCCESS

Always warm up your muscles, joints, and cardiovascular system before performing sprints.

—

Start your foot turnover rate at a moderate pace, gradually increasing to your maximum sprint speed.

—

Adjust or lessen your pace if you feel pain or distress.

—

Always be aware of your surroundings and foot placement when performing sprints.

—

Always perform a cool–down to decrease your heart rate and bring your breathing back to normal.

—

Remember to perform your stretches at the end of the workout.

MEASURING WORKOUT INTENSITY

To measure how hard you really are working, whether it be aerobically or anaerobically, it is valuable to understand how the oxygen is pumped to the working muscles and how much effort you are putting forth.

There are a number of ways to measure the intensity level at which you are working. The assessment tool, 'perceived exertion' or the 'Talk Test' as described in Chapter 1, is one way for you to measure how hard you are working. Monitoring your heart rate is another option for measuring your work intensity and this can be determined by counting your pulse or by wearing a heart rate monitor.

The Heart Rate

When your body starts to move during exercise, the heart must pump a greater volume of blood and more often to provide sufficient oxygen to the working muscles. As the heart becomes stronger it pumps out a greater volume of blood and therefore does not need to beat as often to provide the required oxygen to the body. As you become more fit, and your cardio conditioning improves, you will notice that your heart rate decreases and beats a fewer number of times in one minute.

Taking Your Pulse

The pulse is a measure of your heart beating and can be used as a determination of your fitness level and how hard you are working. It is easy to find your pulse in two areas, either on the side of the neck, just beside the trachea and placing your index finger and/or the middle finger on the carotid artery, or on the underside of the wrist placing your index finger and middle finger on

▼ Taking your pulse

Carotid artery

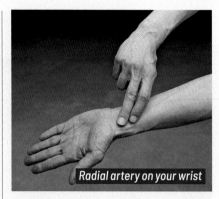
Radial artery on your wrist

▲ Taking your pulse

the radial artery. It is important that you place your fingers lightly on the arteries to feel the pulse in order not to impede the blood flow.

Measuring your resting heart rate can be accomplished without any equipment, simply by finding your pulse while you are sitting quietly or lying down, and then placing your finger on the carotid artery or radial artery. Count the number of beats in 60 seconds. This number is the amount of times your heart pumps blood to the rest of the body and can be used as a base indicator measurement. As you become more physically fit the number of beats in one-minute will reduce because your heart becomes more efficient providing the required oxygen to the body. To measure your training heart rate while exercising, slow down your movement and place your finger on one of the arteries. Take your pulse for 10 or 30 seconds and then multiply by six or two to obtain your training heart rate. The 60-second count is not generally used while exercising because the heart will slow down as soon as you slow or stop moving.

The Training Heart Rate

As you increase your work intensity, your heart will respond by working harder and beating faster. In order to become more physically fit and better conditioned, you need to place increased demands on your heart to beat faster and work at a training heart

VO2 Max (90%-100%):

Training at your limit. You will only be able to sustain this intensity for a very small amount of time, most likely less than 1 minute and you will not be able to talk. Training at this level will enhance your speed and efficiency. This is equivalent to the 10 rating on the Perceived Exertion Scale.

Remember to train at the intensity level specific to your desired outcome and specific to the demand of the exercise you are performing.

Heart Rate Efficiency

The length of time it takes for your pulse to return back to your resting heart rate is a great indicator of your fitness level. As you become increasingly more physically fit, the faster your heart rate will recover back to your resting heart rate after a workout. Also over a period of training weeks, your trained heart becomes stronger and supplies a greater amount of blood to the working muscles with less effort and has to therefore, beat less often. You will be able to perform at a higher level with less effort.

rate level for a determined amount of time. There are a variety of ways to calculate your training heart rate and we have found the most accepted and reliable method is to use the formula 220 minus your age. This will give you your calculated maximum heart rate (MVO2). From there, a percentage rating is allocated to your predicted MVO2, depending on the intensity level you want to train.

If you are 30 years old, your calculated maximum heart rate will be 220 minus 30 or 190 beats in 60 seconds. To determine the intensity level, you are training at or want to achieve, multiply the number 190, by one of the established percentages below. Working at these different training heart rate zones provides specific results. If you want to work at a steady rate for a sufficient amount of time (endurance training), multiply 190 by sixty per cent and seventy per cent (190 x .60 and .70) to give you a training heart rate of 114 to 133 beats in 60 seconds or 19 to 22 beats in 10 seconds. Take your pulse at the carotid artery or radial artery site to obtain the number of times your heart beats in 60 seconds or 10 seconds. Once established, either increase your exercise effort or decrease it in order to match up with the desired training heart rate zone.

Training Heart Rate Zones
Endurance Conditioning (60%–70%):

Training at a moderate rate, developing both cardiovascular and muscular efficiency. Your heart rate increases somewhat, and you will breathe slightly faster. Fat is mostly used as the energy source. This is equivalent to the 4 to 5 rating on the Perceived Exertion Scale.

Aerobic Conditioning (70%-80%):

The training intensity is taken up a notch. Your breathing rate will increase, talking becomes more difficult and you start to sweat. Training at this slightly higher rate assists in improved cardiovascular conditioning, muscular strength, and weight control. The fuel source is both fat and carbohydrates. This is equivalent to the 6 to 7 rating on the Perceived Exertion Scale.

Anaerobic Conditioning (80%-90%):

You are training hard, breathing becomes strenuous, it becomes difficult to talk, and your muscles fatigue quickly. This is the level you will be working at when performing intervals or speed work. Training at this level improves your lung capacity and enhance lactate tolerance. This is equivalent to the 8 to 9 rating on the Perceived Exertion Scale.

Heart Rate Monitors

An alternative to taking your pulse manually is to use a heart rate monitor to help you determine how hard you are working. There are many types of heart rate monitors available and they offer you real-time data while you are training. The basic models record your heart rate at rest and during your training. Also, many heart rate monitors can be pre-programmed to assist training at different workout levels.

An electrode, usually on a band, is positioned either around the chest or the arm and will detect your working heart rate. This information shows up on the corresponding watch allowing you to monitor your intensity level without stopping or slowing down to locate your pulse. Excessive motion and moisture however, may produce imprecise readings.

Some other features many heart rate monitors include are:

- *Time in target zone:* This feature monitors the amount of time you spend exercising within your desired target heart rate zone. Depending on the objective of your training, ideal training times will vary.
- *Recovery heart rate mode:* This records the time it takes for your heart to return to its normal resting rate and is useful for monitoring sprint and interval workouts. You can also use this to evaluate your cardiovascular

fitness, reviewing the length of time it takes for your working heart to return to a resting rate.
- *Speed and distance monitor:* The speed and distance of your run is measured for a specific workout. Generally, a GPS receiver is used for outdoor workouts and a foot pod, measuring stride length, is used for indoor workouts.
- *Fitness Apps:* Many fitness apps are available to upload to your smart phone, tablets, or computer. Specific features allow you to track training statistics and analysis.

The heart rate monitor is a useful tool for you to understand how your heart reacts to exercising and is a guide to access your cardiovascular fitness over a period of time. It does not, though take into account other physiological or psychological factors that can influence your training intensity. Many factors such as stress levels, your health status, the temperature, whether it be very hot or cold, when your last meal was digested, and the natural rhythms of your body will influence your heart rate. Always pay attention to your running intensity, how hard or easy it feels and employ the perceived exertion rating scale as a resource.

OTHER CONSIDERATIONS:

Footwear
Choose running shoes that provide good heel support, have mid-sole flexibility, and adequate sole cushioning for your weight. Go to a reputable sports store with knowledgeable and trained staff and try on running shoes that are designed for your running style and foot structure.

Warm Weather Running
When running in hot weather avoid training in the hottest part of the day.

It is often best to run early in the morning or later in the day after the sun has set, staying away from the direct sunlight. Wear light coloured, light weight clothing made from breathable fabrics and clothing that also repels moisture. To protect your eyes from the sun wear sunglasses or a visor and always remember to apply sunscreen on any exposed skin. Find locations that provide a shady running route. If you run in the night or darker early mornings, wear reflective clothing or carry a flashing light.

Drink water before, during, and after your training. To stay hydrated on long runs, drink eight ounces of water, every one to two hours. Either wear a belt that is capable of holding small water bottles or plan a route that passes by locations where you can refill your water bottle. Also, if you are sweating excessively, include an electrolyte replacement plan to your drinking schedule by adding some Gatorade to your water, (half water, half Gatorade).

When running in warmer temperatures, reduce your exercise training intensity levels initially as your heart rate may increase because of the heat. It generally takes a couple weeks to acclimatize to any major change in temperature. As you get used to the heat, increase the time and intensity of your runs. On hot, humid days substitute outdoor runs with indoor track or treadmill training.

Cold Weather Running

Layering is the key when running in cold weather. For most cold weather running, choose clothing with moisture transport qualities wearing them close to your body, and a breathable wind-proof jacket and pants overtop. For the coldest winter days, wear an additional mid-layer of clothing that fits loose to the body and allows moisture to move away from your skin, but also helps to

Shorten your stride on slippery surfaces

insulate the body. Your body temperature will increase into your run, and in order to reduce the risk of excessive sweating and overheating during your run dress so you feel slightly chilled when you start your run. Be aware of over-dressing and overheating.

To prevent the loss of your body's heat through your head, wear a toque, headband, or balaclava. Keep your hands warm by wearing gloves or mitts and if the sun is shining, remember to wear sunscreen and sunglasses for protection against the glare of the snow on the ground.

It is just as important to hydrate during cold weather runs as it is hot weather runs. For longer runs, fill your water bottle with warm fluids and keep it under your jacket to prevent it from freezing. Remember to hydrate before, during, and after your runs.

If the temperature outside is minus 10° Celsius (15° Fahrenheit) and below, it is extremely windy, or the conditions are icy, a better option is to run indoors

Cecilia Braekhus

REMEMBER TO TAKE EXTRA TIME TO WARM-UP YOUR BODY AND MUSCLES IN COLD WEATHER. YOU MAY WANT TO START BY WALKING BRISKLY FOR 3 TO 5 MINUTES. ALSO TRY WARMING YOUR CLOTHES BY PLACING IN THE DRYER BEFORE HEADING OUT FOR YOUR RUN.

Take extra time to warm up

on a track or a treadmill. Be aware of the terrain you are running on outdoors and keep your feet closer to the ground with a shorter running stride. Stay away from icy areas or packed snow and choose a cleared path or fresh snow, which will provide better traction and lower the risk of slipping. Start by running into the wind. This way you will have the wind at your back on the second half of your run, reducing the chance of getting chilled after you have been sweating. Try to time your runs during the daylight hours and wear bright colours in the snowy weather. If you do run at night, wear reflective clothing or carry a flashing light.

Remember to take extra time to warm-up your body and muscles in cold weather. You may want to start by walking briskly for 3 to 5 minutes. Also try warming your clothes by placing in the dryer before heading out for your run.

Performing roadwork within your training schedule will improve your cardiovascular fitness, breathing rate, and leg strength. Choose an appropriate running program specific to your fitness level and attempt to complete two to three times per week. Roadwork is also incorporated in the B.I.T.S. (Boxing Interval Training System), Chapter 10.

MEDICINE BALL WORKOUTS

MEDICINE BALL TRAINING CHALLENGES REACTION TIME, STRENGTH, BALANCE, AND AGILITY. THE BALL CAN BE LIFTED, PUSHED, PRESSED, THROWN, OR TOSSED. IT IS ONE OF THE MOST VERSATILE STRENGTH TRAINING TOOLS.

Strength training with the medicine ball

The medicine ball allows for a greater range of motion at the joint areas and involves more muscles and movement than when working with just hand weights or machines. Your centre of gravity is constantly changing when moving the ball around, challenging your stability and dexterity. The medicine ball delivers an incredibly dynamic, effective workout for core muscle development and upper body and lower conditioning. The classic piece of equipment can be a wonderful tool for your strength training.

The origins of boxing can be traced back to ancient Greece and Rome. Those brutal matches though, hardly resemble the intricate physical science that boxing has become today. The medicine ball also has an ancient history. It was nearly 3000 years ago that the Greek physician, Hippocrates had his patients toss primitive sand filled sacs around to develop musculature for injury prevention and rehabilitation. Persian wrestlers trained using their version of a medicine ball to build strength and stamina to get ready for a match. The medicine ball is still used today and has evolved over many centuries.

As strength training evolved for boxing, exercises were designed to condition the abdominal muscles. One 'old school' exercise was to simulate body punches by tossing a leather medicine ball to the abdominal region of the boxer. It was thought that this type of drill would develop stronger abdominal muscles to absorb the body punches. Thankfully there are many more effective exercises that do not involve throwing a ball to somebody's mid-section.

The Ball

Traditionally the medicine ball was made from leather and now is designed with such materials as rubber, vinyl, and neoprene for the outer covering. The balls are filled with materials such as sand, steel shot, and gel-filled poly-vinyl chloride shells. The weights range from 1 to 14 kg (2 to 30 lb).

Modern medicine balls

WORKING WITH THE MEDICINE BALL

Grip the Ball
Ensure you have a firm grip on the ball. As you execute the moves maintain proper muscle alignment and keep the core muscles engaged.

How to Breathe
Remember to exhale or breathe out on exertion, when you press or push the medicine ball away from your body. Inhale when returning the ball back to the starting position or on the relaxation phase of the exercise.

Ball Selection
Choose a medicine ball weight that allows you to complete 8 to 15 repetitions of the exercise for upper body exercises and 10 to 20 repetitions for lower body exercises. Traditionally 2-3 sets of the exercises are performed. A better choice for the exercises requiring the ball to be placed on the floor is a larger sized ball as this will offer a more stable base.

Which Level?
The medicine ball exercises are rated as basic, intermediate, and advanced. Select the appropriate exercises for your fitness level. When working with the medicine ball all movement should be smooth and controlled.

UPPER BODY EXERCISES

Standing Medicine Ball Twist
(Basic - Intermediate)
Targeted muscles: Deltoids, obliques, abdominus recti, latissimus dorsi, trapezius

Hold the medicine ball in front of the body at shoulder level with the arms fully extended. Keep the arms extended as you rotate your body as far as you can to one side. Then rotate toward the other side. This is a single repetition. The shoulder muscles fatigue first, so choose a medicine ball at a lighter weight. For added intensity rotate to the side further and swivel onto the ball of the opposite foot.

Staggered Push-Ups *(Advanced)*
Targeted muscles: pectoralis major, triceps, serratus anterior

Push-ups on the medicine ball provide a slightly unstable surface, making it a more challenging push-up than one performed on the floor. With one hand on the ball and the other on the floor, obtain a push-up position. The muscles of the shoulders and the rotator cuff are required to stabilize the torso as the push-up is being executed. Ensure you perform the push-ups in a slow and controlled manner, exhaling on exertion, (or when you push-up), and inhaling as you lower your body. If you are just starting out, reduce the stress on the shoulders by modifying the push-up and placing both knees on the floor. Select a medicine ball that is larger in size to give you a more stable base. Perform the required numbered of push-ups on one side then switch the ball to the other hand and repeat.

▼ Standing Medicine Ball Twist (A-B-C)

A Start

B Rotate to the side

C Rotate to the opposite side

▼ Staggered Push-Ups (A-B)

Up position

Down position

The Boxer's Push-Up
(Advanced)

Targeted muscles: pectoralis major, triceps, serratus anterior

This advanced push-up requires extra strength and control through the core, arms, and shoulders to maintain perfect balance. Both hands are placed on the medicine ball and the body is in the push-up position. Maintain a strong body with the abdominals held tight and the hands held close together. As you lower the body toward the ground keep the elbows pointing back and take a breath in. Next raise the body, extending the arms and exhale. Once again, execute the push-ups from both knees if you are having difficulty maintaining a strong core. Select a medicine ball that is larger in size to give you a more stable base.

▼ The Boxer's Push-Up (A-B)

Start

Stay balanced as you lower your body

CORE STRENGTH EXERCISES

Medicine Ball Crunch *(Basic)*
Targeted muscles: abdominus recti

▼ Medicine Ball Crunch (A-B)

Start position

Hold the medicine ball with both hands close to the chest. Feet stay on the floor with the knees bent and eyes look up toward the ceiling. Raise the upper body, head, and shoulder blades off the floor as a unit, pause, contracting the abdominals tight and then slowly lower to the floor.

Lift your head and shoulders in a smooth motion

▼ Seated Bent Knee Tuck (A-B)

Squeeze the ball firmly between your knees

Pull your knees towards your chest

▼ Overhead Pull-Up (A-B)

Start with the arms extended above your head

Finish with the ball by your legs

Seated Bent Knee Tuck *(Basic)*

Targeted muscles: abdominus recti, oblique abdominus externus, tensor fascia lata, rectus femoris

Sit on the floor with the medicine ball placed between your knees. Keep the body in an upright position and lean back on your hands. Squeeze the ball firmly between your knees and then pull your knees and the ball in toward your chest. Next lower your knees and feet toward the floor. This is one repetition.

Overhead Pull-Up *(Intermediate)*

Targeted muscles: abdominus recti, anterior deltoid, tensor fascia lata, rectus femoris

Lie flat on your back on the floor with the arms extended overhead, knees bent, and feet on the floor. Hold the ball firmly between your hands and keep the arms extended as you sit up. Slowly return to the floor, lowering the head, shoulders, arms, and the ball in unison.

Side Pullover Sit-Up *(Intermediate)*

Targeted muscles: abdominus recti oblique abdominus externus, pec minor, anterior and medial deltoids

Lie flat on the floor holding the medicine ball over the left shoulder with the ball is resting on the floor. As you sit up, pull the ball across the body and reach out to the right side. Return to the start position and touch the ball on the floor by the shoulder. Look at the ball as it goes from one side to the other, keeping the movement smooth. Execute the pullover on one side for the full number of repetitions and then duplicate the same number of repetitions on the other side, starting at the opposite shoulder.

▼ Side Pullover Sit-Up (A-B)

Hold the ball close to your shoulder

Execute the pullover

▼ Medicine Ball Abdominal Press (A-B)

Start with your knees in

Press your leg long

Medicine Ball Abdominal Press (Intermediate)

Targeted muscles: abdominus recti, oblique abdominus externus, tensor fascia lata, rectus femoris

Sit on the floor holding the medicine ball at chest level. Start with the knees close to the chest and then slowly press both legs out holding then just above the floor. Let the body move slightly backward as your legs are extended out. Pause and then pull the knees back toward the chest. Repeat.

Option: To make this exercise easier, do not hold onto the ball. Lean back and place your hands on the floor behind you with your fingertips facing forward and the elbows slightly bent.

Medicine Ball Cycle (Intermediate)

Targeted muscles: abdominus externus, abdominus recti, oblique abdominus, rectus femoris

Sit on the floor holding the medicine ball tight to your chest. Move the legs in a cycling motion as you rotate your upper body. Bring the left knee in toward the chest and rotate the body to the left. Aim to touch the right elbow on the left thigh. Simultaneously extend the right leg just above the floor. Switch legs and bring the right knee toward

the chest rotating your upper body to the right, touching the left elbow to the right thigh and extending the left leg above the floor. The movement of the ball from the left side to the right side and the right side to the left side (with the legs cycling) counts as one repetition. Ensure the movement is a slow, controlled, and a continuous motion.

▼ Medicine Ball Cycle (A-B)

Rotate the ball to the side

Move the legs in a cycling motion

Medicine Ball Plank (Advanced)

Targeted muscles: abdominus recti, oblique abdominus externus, serratus anterior

Place both hands on the medicine ball and obtain the push-up position. Maintain a strong core by pulling the abs up toward the spine. The medicine ball plank is more difficult to perform than a regular plank because the medicine ball provides a very unstable base. More abdominal muscle fibres will be activated to maintain your balance when using the ball as compared to supporting yourself on the floor with your elbows and forearms. Select a medicine ball that is larger in size to give you a more stable base.

Option: Plank without the medicine ball. Bend your elbows at ninety degrees with your body weight on your forearms. Keep your body flat, legs long, and your shoulders directly above your elbows.

▼ Medicine Ball Plank

▼ Roll-Up and Knee Tuck (A-B)

Start position

Raise arms and legs in a smooth motion

Roll-Up and Knee Tuck *(Advanced)*
Targeted muscles: abdominus recti, tensor fascia lata, rectus femoris, quadriceps

Lie flat on your back with your legs extended long. Hold the medicine ball between both hands above your head and slightly off the floor. Raise your arms and the ball at the same time as you raise your body and bring both knees in toward the chest. Reach the ball over the knees as if to hug them. Return slowly to the start position. Lower the body and arms at the same time as you extend the legs to a position just above the floor. Hold the legs extended a few centimetres off of the floor until the next repetition.
Option: *Single Leg Roll-Up and Knee Tuck* – If this movement is too difficult, tuck one knee at a time and allow the opposite leg to rest on the floor. Alternate your legs with each repetition.

V-Ups *(Advanced)*
Targeted muscles: abdominus recti, tensor fascia lata, rectus femoris, quadriceps

This challenging move incorporates raising the upper body, arms, and medicine ball simultaneously while lifting both legs. Start with the body flat on the floor, legs extended long, and arms overhead. Hold the medicine ball with a firm grip. In one movement, lift the upper body and the legs into a V-position, reaching the ball to touch the feet. Pause and then lower the medicine ball, arms, body, and legs in a controlled, smooth manner back to the floor. Ensure that the legs are kept together and the arms stay straight and close to the head throughout the movement.
Option: *Single Leg V-Up* - An easier option is a single leg V-up. Leave one straight leg on the floor while you lift the other leg at the same time you raise the body and arms. Reach and touch the ball to the elevated foot. The single leg V-up is easier as less stress is placed on the lower back muscles.

▼ V-Ups (A-B + Single leg V-Up option)

Start position

Lift the body and legs into a V-position

Single leg V-up option

LOWER BODY EXERCISES

Forward Lunges (Basic)
Targeted muscles: gluteus maximus, quadriceps, biceps femoris

Hold the medicine ball at chest level and feet side-by-side, shoulder width apart. Take a step forward with one foot, planting the heel on the floor first. Lower your body weight onto the front leg ensuring the knee does not bend past 90 degrees. Hold your core tight and perpendicular to your front thigh as the back knee bends toward the floor, acting as a stabilizer. Push off the front foot firmly returning back to the start position. Repeat stepping forward with your other foot. This counts as one repetition.

▼ Forward Lunges (A-B)

Lower your body weight on the front leg

Power Squats (Advanced)
Targeted muscles: gluteus maximus, gluteus medius, quadriceps, soleus, gastroncnemius, plantaris

Stand with the feet shoulder-width apart and the ball held in tight at chest level. Keep the back straight, shoulders relaxed, and your head facing forward. Lower into a squat position, with your body weight centred through the feet and slightly onto your heels. Pause in the squat and then blast upward, pushing off the floor and extending the legs. When landing, roll through the balls of the feet and return to the squat position.

▼ Power Squats (A-B)

Lower into a squat position

Blast upward

▼ 180s (A-B-C)

180s – Start in a squat position

Drive up into the air

Land in a squat position

180s (Advanced)
Targeted muscles: gluteus maximus, gluteus medius, quadriceps, soleus, gastroncnemius, plantaris

This explosive move starts from a squat position with your feet positioned slightly wider than your shoulders. Hold the medicine ball at chest level, looking straight ahead with the shoulders relaxed and down, and placing your weight through the centre of your feet. Using the power of your legs, drive up into the air and turn 180 degrees landing in a squat position facing in the opposite direction. Jump up and return to the start position. Land softly and controlled, allowing the knees to absorb the impact. Jump and rotate in the air turning to the right and land. Then jump up, turning left and land. This counts as one repetition.

FULL BODY EXERCISES

Woodchopper (Intermediate)
Targeted muscles: gluteus maximus, quadriceps, biceps femoris, abdominus recti, erector spinae, oblique abdominus externus, latissimus dorsi, deltoids, biceps brachii

Standing with your feet slightly larger than shoulder width apart and your arms extended, hold the medicine ball overhead. Bend the body forward, mimicking a wood chopping motion maintaining a secure grip on the ball. Allow the ball to fall toward the floor and between your legs and then quickly bring the back up to the start position. This is one repetition.

▼ Woodchopper (A-B)

Hold the ball overhead

Swing the ball between your legs

Mountain Climber (Intermediate)
Targeted muscles: gluteus maximus, quadriceps, biceps femoris, abdominus recti, erector spinae

Place the medicine ball on the floor, with your hands firmly gripping the ball. Lower your body and perform a running leg motion, moving your feet back and forth. Bring a knee in close to the body and extend the opposite leg in a rapid motion. Right foot back, then left foot back is one repetition. Select a medicine ball that is larger in size to give you a stable base.

▼ Mountain Climber (A-B)

Have a firm grip on the ball

Alternate your legs in a running motion

Rock 'n' Roll (Advanced)
Targeted muscles: gluteus maximus, quadriceps, biceps femoris, abdominus recti, anterior deltoid, tensor fascia lata, rectus femoris

This challenging move works all the major muscle groups. Start lying on your back with your arms extended overhead holding a medicine ball. Tuck the knees in toward your chest, rolling backward and building momentum.

▼ Rock 'n' Roll (A-B-C)

Roll backward and build momentum

Roll up to your feet

Finish standing straight

Rock the body and swing the arms and ball forward. Roll up and finishing the move standing straight. Reverse the movement, lowering slowly into a squat, then onto your buttocks and returning onto your back. Your arms extend overhead with the ball.

Medicine Ball Burpees (*Advanced*)
Targeted muscles: gluteus maximus, quadriceps, biceps femoris, abdominus recti, erector spinae, pectoralis major, serratus anterior, triceps

With the medicine ball on the floor, rest both hands on the ball, lean forward and place your weight on the ball. From a squat position thrust your legs backward as far as possible, keeping the body long and strong, and hands steady on the ball. Jump in returning to the squat position and then jump into the air. Place your hands on the ball again ready to repeat the burpee. Select a medicine ball that is larger in size to give you a stable base.

Place your weight on the ball

Thrust your legs backward

Jump in

▼ Medicine Ball Burpees (A-B-C-D)

Jump up

KEYS TO SUCCESS

Ensure you have a secure grip on the ball.

—

Reduce the weight of the ball if you feel any pain in the joint areas.

—

Use a larger sized medicine ball when balancing on the ball.

—

Exhale on exertion or when pressing or pushing the medicine ball away from the body.

—

Inhale when returning the medicine ball back to the start position.

MEDICINE BALL WORKOUTS

Three medicine ball routines are described below. Choose the appropriate ball size and routine, making modifications to the exercises as required. Complete one set of the routine, building up to the maximum repetitions. As you become stronger, add another set. Adjust the number of repetitions you perform in each set. Repeat two to three sets.

Warm-up your muscles by shadow-boxing for two to three minutes before starting a workout.

Exercise	Ball Size	Repetitions
BASIC		
Standing Medicine Ball Twist	3 – 5 kg (6-10 lb)	8 – 12
Forward Lunges	4 – 7 kg (8-15 lb)	10 – 20
Overhead Pull-Ups	3 – 5 kg (6-10 lb)	10 – 15
Seated Bent Knee Tuck	3 – 5 kg (6-10 lb)	10 – 15
Side Pullover Sit-Up	3 – 5 kg (6-10 lb)	10 – 15
Medicine Ball Crunch	3 – 5 kg (6-10 lb)	10 – 20
Woodchopper	3 – 4 kg (6-8 lb)	10 – 12

Take a one-minute break in between each set and repeat the routine.

Exercise	Ball Size	Repetitions
INTERMEDIATE		
Staggered Push-Ups	large	10 - 12
Roll-Up and Knee Tuck	3 - 4 kg (6-8 lb)	10 - 15
Medicine Ball Abdominal Leg Press	3 - 5 kg (6-10 lb)	10 - 15
Power Squats	3 - 5 kg (6-10 lb)	10 - 15
Medicine Ball Cycle	3 - 5 kg (6-10 lb)	10 - 15
Medicine Ball Plank	large	30 - 60 sec.
Mountain Climber	large	20 - 30

Take a one-minute break in between each set and repeat the routine.

Exercise	Ball Size	Repetitions
ADVANCED		
Boxer's Push-up	large	8 - 12
Rock 'n' Roll	3 - 4 kg (6-8 lb)	10 - 12
V-Ups	3 - 4 kg (6-8 lb)	10 -15
Side Pullover Sit-Up	3 - 5 kg (6-10 lb)	10 - 15
Medicine Ball Cycle	3 - 5 kg (6-10 lb)	10 - 15
Medicine Ball Crunch	3 - 5 kg (6-10 lb)	10 - 20
180s	3 - 4 kg (6-8 lb)	12 - 15
Medicine Ball Burpees	large	12 - 15

Take a one-minute break in between each set and repeat the routine.

HOW OFTEN SHOULD I TRAIN WITH THE MEDICINE BALL?

It is optimal to perform functional strength training exercises three to four times per week, allowing a rest day in between workouts. Follow the above medicine ball strength training routines as above. Medicine ball training is also included in the B.I.T.S. (Boxing Interval Training System), Chapter 10.

ACTIVE MUSCLE STRETCHES

GOOD FLEXIBILITY IS ESSENTIAL FOR EVERYDAY LIVING AND WITH RESPECT TO SPORTS AND TRAINING, IT IS ESPECIALLY VALUABLE IN ENHANCING ATHLETIC PERFORMANCE. OPTIMAL MUSCLE LENGTH AND JOINT MOBILITY PROVIDES BETTER COORDINATION, MUSCLE CONTROL, AND ALLOWS FOR PROPER EXECUTION OF MOVEMENTS.

Including a stretching session in all of your workouts gives you a sound and an effective training program. A regular stretching program is essential to maintain the best possible conditioned and flexible musculature and the optimal range of motion at your joints.

BENEFITS OF STRETCHING

Stretching increases blood flow to the muscles and assists with improved circulation. Increased blood flow to the muscle tissues supplies essential nutrients to working muscles and helps

to reduce muscle soreness. The more conditioned and subtle your muscles and tendons are, the better they can manage intense physical demands.

Flexible joints and muscles help to minimize the risk of injury. It is important that the muscles surrounding the joints are able to move through a full range of motion without placing undue strain on the ligaments, tendons, and capsular structures. When muscles are unable to extend all the way, you are increasing the risk of joint pain, strains and muscular damage. Also, strong muscles that are pliable and limber can withstand any additional stress resulting from intense training. A strong muscle that is rigid and inflexible will tear resulting in soreness and discomfort.

Stretching and flexibility promotes the maintenance of good posture, assisting in a better quality of everyday life activities. As well, stretching can help the muscles relax and relieve any tension.

Reduction of Muscle Soreness
The lactic acid that builds up in the muscle tissue when you are working out will often cause soreness and fatigue in your muscles. By stretching these muscles, the blood circulation to that area is increased and helps to flush out the lactic acid build up. By lowering the occurrence of muscle soreness, you are more likely to stick with your workout schedule.

STRETCH EVERY DAY

For overall physical fitness, stretching needs to occur on a regular basis. Focus on the key areas that you are training and include more stretches for these areas. Be aware of the muscles that are tight and spend additional time stretching them. Often people will not stretch a muscle or joint area until they actually

Flexible muscles enhance athletic performance

TAKE THE TIME TO STRETCH THE MUSCLES THAT HAVE BECOME TOO TIGHT OR INFLEXIBLE

feel stiff or sore. Aim to find the balance between the strength of a muscle and the extensibility of that same muscle. Due to sport-specific demands, poor postural habits, or previous injuries muscular imbalance may be evident. Take the time to stretch the muscles that have become too tight or inflexible. Stretch both sides of your body making sure that the range of motion and extensibility are as equal as possible on each side. It is most beneficial to perform stretching exercises at the end of your workout, however, you may be tired and less enthusiastic to do so and will forgo your stretching. Over a period of time this often leads to the muscles becoming less pliable and a reduced range of motion at your joint areas. Stretch to keep both your mobility and independence, and always make time to stretch with every workout.

TYPES OF FLEXIBILITY TRAINING

Static Stretching

Static stretching exercises are safe and are used to increase the range of motion at a joint. Slowly stretch to the farthest point and hold the stretch. There should not be any pain associated with this stretch. The stretch is held for a brief period of time, (30 to 60 seconds), and then released back to the starting muscle length.

Dynamic Stretching

Dynamic stretching prepares the body for movement and is sport specific. It combines both flexibility and strength, taking the muscle through a large range of motion and focusing on the movement patterns required for training. These exercises are performed in a controlled manner and at faster rate than static stretching. Do not bounce or force the stretch and hold the stretch for a very short period of time, (5 -10 seconds).

Passive Stretching

Passive stretching is created by an external force, like a mechanical device, a partner, or gravity causing the muscle to stretch. The muscles around the joint remain inactive and relaxed.

Proprioceptive Neuromuscular Facilitation (PFN Stretching)

PFN Stretching is also called "active assist stretching", increases range of motion and flexibility and originated as a rehabilitation technique. It is important to warm up the muscles before performing this type of stretching. To execute, lengthen a muscle close to its maximum level, (static stretch), then contract the muscle in that lengthened state. This contraction is held for 10 – 20 seconds and then relaxed for 20 seconds. During the relaxation, slowly increase the stretch. Another hold-relax stretch is then performed.

Pre-Activity Stretching

The purpose of a pre-activity stretch is to warm-up the muscles and joint areas and not necessarily to increase the length of the muscle. Always warm up your muscles and joint areas before performing stretches by increasing your heart rate. This can be accomplished by walking around, performing large arm circles, and leg lifts, and imitating the training you will be doing later, for about five minutes. Perform dynamic stretches, taking the muscles through a large range of motion and reducing any tightness.

Post-Activity Stretching

As previously mentioned, it is extremely beneficial to stretch at the end of a workout. The purpose of a post-activity stretch is to lengthen the muscles you have been training. Stretching promotes blood flow to these muscles assisting in the removal of by-products such as lactic acid. Hold a post-activity stretch for 30 to 60 seconds, moving into the stretch until a mild tension is felt in the muscle, pause and then try to reach slightly further into the stretch. Perform static stretches, always moving gently and slowly into the stretch. If the stretch feels painful, then you have moved too far or too fast into the stretch. Release the stretch and hold where there is not any pain. Focus on the muscle you are trying to lengthen and do not place any stress on the associated joints. Never bounce or force a stretch, as this can cause small tears in the muscle fibres, resulting in pain and scar tissue. Always breathe during your stretch and never hold your breath. Breathe in as you prepare for the stretch and breathe out as you move into your stretch.

STRETCHING FROM HEAD TO TOE

Sixteen stretches are described below. Perform stretches for all of your muscle groups, spending additional time stretching the muscles you have trained hard and any muscles that feel tight.

Neck Stretch
Targeted muscles:
levator scapula, upper trapezius

Either sitting or standing, bend your head to one side and slightly forward. Place the opposite hand lightly on the side of your head, and gently pull downward. Hold the stretch for 30 seconds. Release and perform the stretch tilting your head to the other side.

▼ Neck Stretch (A-B)

A
Tilt your head to one side

B
Gently stretch on opposite side

▼ Upper Back and Shoulder Stretch (A-B)

A
Keep your arm straight

B
Bend at the elbow and press back

Upper Back and Shoulder Stretch
Targeted muscles: *trapezius, rhomboid, teres minor, teres major, infraspinatus, posterior deltoid*

To stretch the upper back, extend one arm and bring it in front of your body. Keep the shoulders square and relaxed, holding onto the elbow area with your other hand. Take a breath and as you exhale gently press the arm toward your body. Hold the stretch for 30 seconds. Release. Next bend the arm at your elbow, inhale and then exhale pressing the arm across your chest toward the other shoulder. Allow the shoulder to roll forward slightly. This stretches out the rear deltoid muscle of the shoulder. Hold the stretch for 30 seconds. Release. Perform both stretches with the other arm.

▼ Pull Back Lat Stretch

Exhale as you sit back

Pull Back Lat Stretch
Targeted muscles: *latissimus dorsi, posterior deltoid, infraspinatus*

Standing, grasp a secure object that is fixed to the floor or ground with both hands at approximately waist level. Breathe in, and then exhale as you sit back allowing the arms to fully extend, stretching through the latissimus dori and posterior deltoid. Try shifting your weight slightly to one side for a further stretch in the back region. Hold the stretch for 30 seconds breathing naturally.

Chest and Shoulder Stretch
Targeted muscles: *pectoralis major, pectoralis minor, anterior deltoid*

To stretch the chest and shoulder muscles, stand with your head facing straight forward and your neck and

▼ Chest and Shoulder Stretch

Keep your neck and shoulders relaxed

shoulders relaxed. Extend your arms behind your back and hold your hands together by interlacing the fingers. Inhale, pull the shoulder blades toward each other and lift the arms up slightly. Now exhale and lower the arms down slowly. Hold the stretch for 30-seconds.

Overhead Triceps Stretch
Targeted muscles:
triceps, deltoid, rotator cuff

The triceps, deltoids, and rotator cuff are all stretched with this exercise. Both arms start in the overhead position. Look forward with the head in a frontal neutral position. Bend one arm back with the elbow pointing toward the ceiling. Try to place the palm of the hand or your fingers near the centre of your back, between the shoulder blades. Place your other hand on the elbow, breathe in and then as you breathe out, press down on the elbow slightly moving the hand down the back. Hold the stretch for 30 seconds. Release the stretch. Repeat on the other arm.

▼ Chest and Biceps Stretch

Allow your muscles to relax completely

Chest and Biceps Stretch
Targeted muscles:
pectoralis major, pectoralis minor, biceps, rotator cuff, deltoids

Standing by a wall, place your bent arm at shoulder height against the wall. Breathe in, and then exhale slowly as you turn your body away from the wall. To target the upper chest muscles place

▼ Kneeling Forearm Stretch (A-B)

A

Arms directly under your shoulders

B

Press the palms of your hands into the ground

the arm further down on the wall, and to target the lower chest muscle place your arm in a position that is slightly higher on the wall. Hold the stretch for 30 to 60 seconds. Release the stretch. Repeat on the other arm.

Kneeling Forearm Stretch
Targeted muscles: *brachioradialis, palmaris longus, flexor carpi radialis*

Kneeling with your arms directly positioned under your shoulders, press the palms of your hands into the ground with the fingers spread apart. Lift one hand and rotate it outward, keeping the fingers spread. Press your palm into the ground and circle your arm at the shoulder joint slowly in one direction for about 10 seconds and then change direction. Breathe normally. Release the stretch and repeat on the

▼ Overhead Triceps Stretch

Front view

Back view

▼ Alternate

Standing forearm stretch

other arm. *Alternate:* This stretch may be executed while you are standing or sitting by holding onto the palm of one hand and lightly pressing backward. Hold the stretch for 30 seconds. Release the stretch. Repeat on the other arm.

Core Side Stretch

Targeted muscles: *rectus abdominus, obliques, latissimus dorsi*

Stand with the feet shoulder width apart, hipbones parallel to the ground, abdominal muscles held tight, and your knees slightly bent. Inhale, and then stretch your arm overhead, exhaling as you reach your arm in a semi-circle and bending your body to the side. Stretch from your fingertips right through to your hipbone. Breathe normally, holding the side stretch for 30 to 60 seconds. Take a breath in and then exhale reaching up and returning to the start position. Repeat on the other side.

▼ Core Side Stretch

Gently stretch to the side

A — Pull both knees to your chest

B — Keep one knee by the chest as you extend your other leg

C — Keep one foot on the ground, with bent knee

▲ Lower Back Stretch (A-B-C)

Lower Back Stretch

Targeted muscles:
erector spinae, gluteals

To stretch your lower back and gluteal area, lie on your back with your knees bent and both feet on the ground. Breathe in, and then exhale as you pull both of your knees in toward your chest. Hold behind your knees. Hold the stretch for 30 seconds. Slowly release the legs and place both feet back on the floor. You can also vary the stretch by starting with both knees in by your chest, inhale and then as you exhale extend one leg long on the ground. Hold the stretch for 30 seconds. Bring both legs back to the chest and repeat with the other leg. To reduce the stress on your lower back, just pull one knee in toward the chest with your other foot on the floor.

Pull the knees towards the chest

▲ Supine Piriformis Stretch

Supine Piriformis Stretch

Targeted muscles:
piriformis, gluteals, fascia lata

This stretch help prevent lower back tightening and tension, Start by lying on your back with your knees bent and one foot on the ground. Place the ankle of the other leg on the bent knee. Lift both legs off the ground holding behind the thigh of the lower leg. Inhale and as you exhale, pull your legs in toward the chest. Breathe normally, holding the stretch for 30 seconds. Release and repeat on the other side.

Kneeling Hip Flexor Stretch

Targeted muscles: *hip flexors, quadriceps, groin*

To stretch a tight hip flexor muscle, place one knee on the ground and your opposite foot in front on the ground. Ensure that the front foot is positioned directly under the knee. The hip is

▼ Kneeling Hip Flexor Stretch

Lightly press your hip forward

bent at 90 degrees. Look forward with the head in a frontal neutral position and place both hands on your thigh, keeping your back straight. Inhale and as you breathe out lightly press your hips forward. Hold the stretch for 30 seconds. Release and repeat on the other side.

Standing Quadriceps Stretch
Targeted muscles:
quadriceps, rectus femoris

To stretch the front on your thigh, stand with your back and torso straight and thighs together. Lift one foot backward keeping the knees close together. Take a breath in and hold onto your ankle. Exhale pulling the heel up and toward your buttock. Hold this position for 30 seconds. Gently release and repeat on the other side.

▼ Standing Quadriceps Stretch

Gently lift one foot backward

Exhale as you reach forward

▲ ITB Stretch

ITB Stretch
Targeted muscles:
iliotibial band, tensor fascia lata

This thick band of connective tissue runs along the outer thigh, from the hip area to the knee. When it is not flexible and pliable, the knee joint may be pulled out of alignment and cause inflammation in your hip area. Stand and cross one foot over the opposite foot, keeping the knees soft or

For a deeper stretch keep your legs extended

unlocked. Inhale bending at the waist and exhale as you reach toward the floor. To increase the stretch, centre your weight through the rear leg. Hold this position for 30 seconds. Gently release and switch legs.

Lying Hamstring Stretch
Targeted muscles:
hamstrings, erector spinae, gluteals

Start the hamstring stretch by lying on your back with both knees bent. Lift one leg and hold behind the thigh with both of your hands. Inhale and then exhale while you straighten the leg. Slowly pull the leg toward your body until a slight tension is felt in the hamstring muscle. Hold this position for 30 seconds. Gently release and

▼ Lying Hamstring Stretch (A–B)

Slowly pull your leg toward your body

▼ Standing Calf/Achilles Stretch

Keep your heel on the ground

TO STRETCH THE LOWER AREA OF THE CALF, BEND YOUR BACK KNEE SLIGHTLY AND SHIFT YOUR BODY WEIGHT BACK OVER THE REAR HEEL.

switch legs. For a deeper stretch keep both legs extended long on the ground and lift one leg up and toward your body. Hold for 30 seconds and repeat on the other leg.

Standing Calf/Achilles Stretch
Targeted muscles:
gastrocnemius, Achilles tendon

Stand with one leg forward and one leg back. Inhale and as you bend the front leg forward, exhale, keeping your rear leg straight and your rear heel on the ground. The stretch will be felt in the centre of the calf muscle. To stretch the lower area of the calf, bend your back knee slightly and shift your body weight back over the rear heel. This will stretch through the lower part of the gastrocnemius muscle and the Achilles tendon area of the leg. Hold each position for 30 seconds. Gently release and switch legs.

Kneeling Soleus/Achilles Stretch
Targeted muscles:
soleus, Achilles tendon

Start with one knee on the ground and the opposite foot placed on the ground beside your knee. Position your hands slightly in front of the knee on the ground to assist with balancing. Try to position your heel as close to the knee as possible. Take a breath in, and as you exhale press your heel to the ground and shift your body weight forward slightly onto your hands. Hold this position for 30 seconds. Gently release and switch legs.

▼ Kneeling Soleus/Achilles Stretch

Keep your heel on the ground

STRETCHING ROUTINES

Stretching is an important part of a complete fitness program. It is advisable to cool down and stretch after every workout. Below are two options: an eight-minute stretch routine with 9 exercises and a more extensive 15-minute stretch routine with 16 exercises. Take your time to perform these exercises in the order laid out. Include the 15-minute routine into your training schedule, two to three times per week.

Eight-Minute Stretching Routine
(9 Stretches)

Upper Back and Shoulder Stretch
Pull Back Lat Stretch
Chest and Biceps Stretch
Forearm Stretch
Piriformis Stretch
Kneeling Hip Flexor Stretch
Standing Quadriceps Stretch
Hamstring Stretch
Standing Calf/Achilles Stretch

Fifteen-Minute Stretching Routine
(16 Stretches)

Neck Stretch
Upper Back and Shoulder Stretch
Pull Back Lat Stretch
Chest and Shoulder Stretch
Triceps Stretch
Chest and Biceps Stretch
Forearm Stretch
Core Side Stretch
Lower Back Stretch
Piriformis Stretch
Kneeling Hip Flexor Stretch
Standing Quadriceps Stretch
ITB Stretch
Hamstring Stretch
Standing Calf/Achilles Stretch
Soleus/Achilles Stretch

ULTIMATE BOXING WORKOUT

KEYS TO SUCCESS

Never bounce when you are stretching. Muscles, tendons and ligaments can be stressed and result in injury.

—

Do not force a muscle to overstretch. Once a tension is felt in the muscle, ease off and hold the length where there is not any discomfort.

—

A static stretch, when a muscle is lengthened just beyond its natural length and held for more than 30 seconds, is the safest and most effective method of stretching.

Improvements in your flexibility, muscle length, and joint mobility will be noticeable if you stretch on a regular basis. Remember, stretching should not feel painful. If there is pain associated with your stretches, ensure you are executing the movements correctly. If you have any joint problems or issues with your back or neck consult with your doctor before performing the exercises.

FUEL YOUR FITNESS

WHATEVER SPORTS OR ACTIVITIES YOU ARE INVOLVED IN YOU NEED TO ADHERE TO A GOOD DIET. A DIET FULL OF HIGH-QUALITY NUTRITION AND AVAILABLE FUEL WILL GIVE YOU MAXIMUM FITNESS RESULTS.

Healthy Diet

A healthy diet not only provides a strong foundation to build a healthy lifestyle, it also delivers the energy required for an optimal workout. Our bodies continually undergo a building and renewal cycle on a daily basis and we need to eat good carbohydrates, proteins, and fats each day to provide nutrition for muscle repair, growth, and energy. A healthy and smart diet reduces body fat, (not just a reduction in water), helps to improve cardiovascular health, reduces the risk of heart disease, hypertension, and cancer, and gives energy to perform normal daily activities. It provides the fuel for you to train at an optimal workout level giving you the best possible results. Your performance and power output are definitely dependent on your nutritional habits.

To workout at your optimum and to improve your fitness level include carbohydrates, proteins, and essential fats in your diet everyday. Carbohydrates

are required for energy, proteins are needed to repair and develop musculature, and the essential fats are necessary to assist in the absorption of specific vitamins and minerals, and to regulate hormonal activity.

THE THREE BASIC FUELS

Carbohydrates

Carbohydrates are needed to provide precious energy to continue and finish a workout. Foods consisting of complex carbohydrates have higher fibre contents and break down slower in your system. This provides energy at a slower rate over a longer period of time while you are training. Simple carbohydrates, like white sugar, processed grains, commercial cereals, bananas, and raisins break down quickly and will give a quick burst of energy, but then quickly leave you feeling depleted. When carbohydrates are converted into blood sugar or blood glucose, the hormone insulin, transports the blood glucose to the liver and muscle tissue and it is stored as glycogen. This stored glycogen provides energy for about two hours and then it is converted into fat and stored as fat. Carbohydrates should make up 40 per cent of your daily food intake. Choose complex carbohydrates like apples, grapes, grapefruit, beans, legumes, nuts, seeds, and whole grain cereal, pasta, and bread to eat.

Eat to fuel your workout

Proteins

High effort training means you will be breaking down muscle fibres and you will experience muscle soreness. Protein is necessary in your diet as it assists in repairing the torn muscle fibres, developing new muscle fibre growth, producing hormones, antibodies, vital enzymes, and assists in metabolizing fats. When an adequate amount of protein is ingested you will reduce the amount of muscle soreness experienced after your workout and physiological benefits will be noted. It is on your rest days that the majority of the repairing and new growth of your muscle fibres occurs. Good protein sources are chicken breast, turkey breast, egg whites, tuna, tofu and supplementary protein shakes. Proteins should make up 30 per cent of your daily food intake.

Fats

Specific dietary fats need to be included in your diet. The essential unsaturated fats are known as fatty acids. Omega-3 and omega-6 fatty acids help to regulate a number of your bodily functions like lowering the risk of heart attacks, strokes, and diabetes. Good fat sources are salmon, tuna, olive oil, and flaxseed oil. Saturated fats, such as fried foods and hydrogenated oils should only be eaten in moderation. It is also important to have fatty tissue on and in the body to stay alive. Fat protects the vital organs, stores energy, insulates the body and contributes with the transportation and absorption of some vitamins. Dietary fats should make up to 30 per cent of your daily food intake.

MICRO-NUTRIENTS

The following three nutrients do not give us the basic energy to perform but are necessary in our daily diets.

Vitamins

Vitamins cannot be made within our bodies, so eating a diet including a variety of food types helps to ensure you are getting the sufficient amount and type of vitamins to stay healthy. Thirteen vitamins are necessary for normal growth, regulating essential bodily functions, and building and maintaining bones, teeth, skin, and blood. A deficiency in vitamins can damage your health. Conversely an excess of certain vitamins can also be harmful. Fat-soluble vitamins, like A, D, E, and K, are stored in our bodies within the liver and fatty tissue and can be toxic if taken in high doses. Water-soluble vitamins, like C, B-vitamins and H, are not stored in the body and need to be replenished daily. Vitamin supplements are often recommended in certain medically defined situations such as; a proven vitamin deficiency, a risk of a deficiency, or a reduced capacity to absorb a vitamin. Eating a well-balanced diet provides the most beneficial method of getting the vitamins you need.

Minerals

Minerals are required for our bodies to work properly, to assist with growth and development, and are important for building strong bones and teeth, and having healthy blood, hair, nerve, and muscle function. All minerals are essential for your health and are obtained by eating a variety of nutritious foods and drinking healthy fluids. Mineral such as sodium, potassium, calcium, and magnesium are known as macro-minerals and are needed on a daily basis, and in larger quantities. These specific mineral set up the basis for electrical impulses that travel along your nerves and muscles, and without them athletic performance is compromised. The minerals that are required in smaller amounts and less often, are known as micro-minerals or trace elements and include zinc, copper, iron, iodine, sulphur, and chloride.

Water

In order to survive and keep your body functioning well, it is essential that you include water in your diet. Water is packed with minerals and electrolytes and it keeps you hydrated by replacing what is lost when you sweat and urinate. The body is made up of 50 per cent to 70 per cent water, with the brain being made up of 80 per cent water. Water helps you digest food, dissolves nutrients so they can be absorbed into your blood stream and carries waste products out of your body. Water helps to regulate your body temperature by perspiring. It acts a lubricant for your joints, assists with the digestion of food, production of energy, building of new tissue, and sending electrical communication between the cells enabling your muscles to respond and produce a movement. Salt is often the electrolyte that is lost during training and needs to be replenished. A salty snack, (nuts, lentil chips, sports drink) will assist in your recovery.

The majority of the water in your body is intercellular. The correct fluid balance between the intercellular fluid and the extracellular fluid, (other body liquids like blood plasma, urine, the fluid between the cells, and lymph), must be in balance. If there is too little water in the cell, the cell will shrivel and die. Too much water will cause the cell to burst. You can live without food for two to four weeks, but you can only live without water a matter of days. Always stay hydrated and drink before, during, and after your training. Do not wait until you feel thirsty, as the dehydration process has already started.

Hydration

For optimal workout performance, correct hydration is one of the most important components. Never underestimate how the body can become depleted of fluids during a workout or training session. This is especially true in warm weather.

Hydration Guidelines:
Pre-Exercise: Drink at least 2 cups (16 ounces) of fluids before exercising.

Proper hydration

During Exercise: Drink 5 ounces (about 5 large swallows or gulps) of fluids every 15-20 minutes. Always have your water bottle handy.

Post-Exercise: Replace lost fluids by drinking 16 to 24 ounces (2-3 cups) for every pound of weight you lost during your workout. To confirm the amount of weight loss during the workout, weigh yourself before and after.

Water is the best fluid/beverage to drink to rehydrate before, during, and after workout.

High water content fruits, such as watermelon and grapes are suitable for pre- and post exercising, as well.

BASIC ENERGY REQUIREMENTS

Basic energy requirements are referred to as calories and the term 'calorie' is used to indicate the energy units that are ingested and also used or burned off for basic survival and activity. The caloric content of the three basic fuels are; protein has 4 calories per gram, carbohydrates have 4 calories per gram, and fat has 9 calories per gram.

It is important to know how many calories you are ingesting versus the number of calories you are burning off. The basal metabolic rate (BMR) is the amount of energy expended by humans while they are at rest. This energy, (or the calories burned), sustains the functioning of your vital organs, such as the heart, lungs, kidneys, liver, and intestines. Calories are also expended when performing physical activities. The more intense an activity, the more calories are burned.

To be in a caloric balance, you should eat approximately the same number of calories as the body is using. In this case your body weight will remain stable. If you are in caloric excess, you are consuming more calories than your

The more intense an activity, the more calories are burned

body is utilizing, and these extra calories will be stored as fat and show as a weight gain. If you are in a caloric deficit, you are consuming fewer calories than your body requires to remain at a stable weight, and you would show a weight loss.

The number of calories required for each individual varies based on your age, sex, and activity level. As you get older or if you live a sedentary lifestyle the recommended caloric intake decreases. The more physically active you are, the more calories you need to consume.

Intense training, requires a higher caloric intake

The following chart is categorized into age groups and shows the acceptable number of calories that can be consumed per day for both men and women when performing normal daily activities. If you are more active, an extra 200 to 400 calories can be consumed.

Recommended Calories Per Day For Normal Daily Activity

Men

14-18 years	2200 calories
19-30 years	2400
31-50 years	2200
51 +	2000

Women

14-18 years	1800 calories
19-30 years	2000
31-50 years	1800
51 +	1600

Every person's body is unique and made up of varying proportions of fat, muscle, and bone. Women generally have a smaller bone structure and a lower body mass than men and therefore would require fewer calories for energy. Increased physical activity levels and intense training requires a higher caloric intake to maintain a desired weight or girth measurement. It should also be noted that it takes more calories to sustain muscle tissue than fatty tissue. Someone with a greater muscle mass will be burning more calories performing a similar activity. This is one reason men can generally eat more calories than women and not gain weight. Due to the male hormonal influence, men have a greater muscle mass. By weight training, increases in muscle mass can be attained.

Counting calories sometimes assists you in understanding how much you are consuming. Keep a food diary and record the types of foods and beverages you are eating and drinking. The associated calories will give you a base as to whether you are consuming the correct number of calories to maintain your desired weight. There are a number of on line calorie counters to help you keep track of your caloric intake.

The recommended weight loss per week is about .5 to 1 kg (1 to 2 lb). One kilogram has approximately 7700 calories. By reducing your caloric intake by 500 to 1000 calories per day, or by increasing your physical activity level and burning off 500 to 1000 calories per day you could lose about .5 to 1 kilogram in a week.

VEGAN AND VEGETARIAN DIET

Vegans eliminate all animal products from their diet and this includes dairy, eggs, and honey. Vegetarians eliminate meat, fish, poultry, and products that contain gelatine or other meat-based products. Lacto-vegetarians consume dairy, but no eggs. Ovo-vegetarians eat eggs but not dairy products, and lacto-ovo vegetarians eat both eggs and dairy products.

As a vegan you must be diligent about plant-based protein intake because of the elimination of the

Maximize performance

151

A VEGAN/VEGETARIAN DIET NATURALLY INCLUDES SUFFICIENT CARBOHYDRATES AND FATS TO FUEL FOR TRAINING, AND WITH THE INCLUSION OF GOOD PLANT-BASED PROTEINS A WELL-BALANCED DIET IS REALISTIC.

WHEN TO EAT

Calories provide energy. Try to eat 30% of your total calories between the time you get up and 10 am, then 40% during the mid-day (10 am to 3 pm), and 30% in the early evening (3 pm to 8 pm).

It is important to know how many calories you are ingesting versus the amount of fat burning and muscle building exercises you are performing. When athletes eat the correct number of calories from a variety of food groups, then vitamin/mineral supplements are not required. Athletes, who limit their caloric intake for a sport that requires a specific weight, like boxing, or the elimination a food group because of an intolerance, like lactose, or a principle or belief like being a vegan, may not eat a sufficient number of nutritious calories and may require supplements.

Eating Before Your Workout
Try to eat healthy carbohydrates 2 to 3 hours before your workout, usually about 300 to 500 calories. You will require this food for energy to get you through the workout. Eat food that agrees with your digestive system.

If you are exercising for less than an hour there is no need to eat during

animal-based proteins. It is important to include a good source of plant-based proteins and an adequate amount, (60 to 90 grams per day), in your diet for the development of new muscle growth and muscle tissue repair.

The main concern of not including meat or dairy products is the non-existence of vitamin B12 in your diet. Vitamin B12 is only found in animal-based foods. B12 affects red blood cell production and red blood cells carry the necessary oxygen for endurance workouts. Many cereals and soy milk are fortified with B12 and provide this essential vitamin. A supplement is also an option. Also, plant-based iron is more difficult to absorb into your tissues than animal-based protein, but with the addition of vitamin C it is more easily absorbed. Eating oranges or other citrus foods with iron-fortified foods, such as whole grain cereals, beans, temp, nuts, and soy should provide you with sufficient amounts of iron.

A vegan/vegetarian's diet naturally includes sufficient carbohydrates and fats to fuel for training, and with the inclusion of good plant-based proteins a well-balanced diet is realistic. As always, if you have any concerns about your nutritional status, it is best to consult with your doctor or a registered sports nutritionist.

Choose your calories carefully

Eat a well balanced diet

the workout. You will just want to ensure you stay hydrated by drinking small sips of water often. If you were unable to eat before a workout, you may choose dried fruits, sport gels, or sport drinks with protein as fuel during your performance. When training over an extended period of time, plan to eat 50 to 100 calories of carbohydrates about every half hour to supply you with sufficient fuel for a good performance.

Eating After Your Workout

Ideally, try to eat some recovery carbohydrates and proteins within 30 to 60 minutes after training. The carbohydrates will replace the depleted muscle glycogen and the protein will repair the damaged muscle fibres. This is especially important for athletes who are training or competing again within six hours. Absorption of nutrients occurs up to 24 hours after a workout, although at a slower rate and if you have a full day to recover before your next workout, you do not have to be preoccupied with refuelling immediately. There are sport drinks, and gels that offer a good carbohydrate/protein ratio of 4:1. An easy choice is chocolate milk, which contains both carbohydrates and protein. Vegans could choose a soy or almond milk option. Also, you can combine a carbohydrate like whole wheat bread (2 slices), with a protein like turkey (2 ounces) for a satisfactory refuelling, approximately 250 to 400 calories.

WHEN TRAINING OVER AN EXTENDED PERIOD OF TIME, PLAN TO EAT 50 TO 100 CALORIES OF CARBOHYDRATES ABOUT EVERY HALF HOUR TO SUPPLY YOU WITH SUFFICIENT FUEL FOR A GOOD PERFORMANCE.

KEY POINTS TO REMEMBER

Start the day by eating a healthy breakfast.

—

Eat a nutritious midday meal.

—

Snack on healthy food choices.

—

Eat a smaller evening meal.

—

Eat carbohydrates 2 to 3 hours before your training.

—

After your workout, eat carbohydrates with some protein.

—

Include some essential fatty acids in your daily diet.

—

Stay hydrated drinking 8 to 10 glasses of water per day.

A Well-Balanced Diet

Without a well-balanced diet, your body is unable to meet the demands of a training regimen. Carbohydrates are needed for energy, protein for muscle growth and repair, and fats for providing essential nutrients and protection from diseases. By following a good diet, your workout performance will improve, muscle soreness will be reduced, and you will become stronger, leaner, and more physically fit. Before going on a diet, consult with your doctor or a nutritional specialist. Be wary of fad diets, as often they do not provide the necessary nutrients and energy.

B.I.T.S

BOXING INTERVAL TRAINING SYSTEM

THE BOXING INTERVAL TRAINING SYSTEM (B.I.T.S.) BRINGS ALL THE ELEMENTS OF BOXING TRAINING TOGETHER AND PRESENTS VARIOUS TRAINING OPTIONS.

Five different workout options are described and depending on your current fitness level, past experience, and training objectives select the appropriate workout. Always remember to warm-up before your workouts, use the Perceived Exertion Chart (Chapter 1) to ensure you are training at the desired level, and take time to cool down.

B.I.T.S.

WORKOUT ONE
The Basic Workout is most beneficial for the novice fitness boxer and it is a workout that can easily compliment your existing training program.

WORKOUT TWO
The Contender Workout Program, adds more intensity to your training and requires a greater commitment to train like a boxer. Additional training elements are added to this workout and the skill level is increased. This is a 10-week workout program, five days a week.

WORKOUT THREE
The Champs Workout Program cranks up the complexity of the drills and the intensity of the training are pushed to the maximum and you will require passion and dedication. This is a 12-week workout program, six days a week.

WORKOUT FOUR
The 12-Round Challenge gives you a chance to test your punching ability and endurance. This workout provides a non-jump rope routine.

WORKOUT FIVE
The 15-Round Knockout provides an authentic experience of old school boxing training.

THE BASIC WORKOUT

3-Day/Week Program
The Basic Workout is a great introduction to the Boxing Interval Training System. It is designed so you can integrate boxing training into your current fitness schedule. Perform the Basic Workout three days per week, every other day. This workout includes heavy bag, jumping rope, shadowboxing, focus mitt training, and medicine ball workouts. The minimal pieces of equipment required are boxing gloves, a heavy bag, and a jump rope.

Shadowboxing Warm-Up
(1 x 3-minute round)
Shadowboxing warms up your working muscles and prepares you mentally to work on the different bags and on punch mitts. It also re-orientates you to the proper execution of the punches. Ensure there is adequate space to move around and throw your punches. If a

Shadowboxing warm-up

mirror is available visually check to make sure your hands are held high, your body position is in the classic boxing stance, and your punches are crisp and clean. Always return the hands back to protect your chin. Add movement with your feet, head, and body keeping balanced and executing your punches smoothly.

During the one-minute rest, stretch out any muscles that feel tight. Refer to Chapter 8 for specific exercises. Loosen up the shoulders, hip flexors, and legs.

Shadowboxing
(1 x 3-minute round)
Throw your punches with a little more intensity. Move around and mix up the punches, moving forward and backward, and side-to-side. Develop smooth transitions both for your punches and your footwork. Balance is the key and weight transfer should be effortless. After throwing a variety of straight punches, start to put together punch combinations. Focus on your punching technique until it becomes second nature. Get used to working for a full three-minutes and pace yourself working at a perceived exertion of 5 to 6. If you want more information on shadowboxing refer to Chapter 2.

Jump Rope
(3 x 3-minute rounds)
Start by jumping at a moderate pace keeping the footwork basic. As you become more experienced increase your jumping intensity. This can be accomplished by moving at a faster pace or by performing more intricate footwork, such as scissors, jumping jacks and even adding some sprints *(refer to Chapter 3)*. The goal is to jump for three minutes straight, take a one-minute break, and then repeat jumping two more times with a one-minute break. This one-minute break gives you time to stretch out tight calf muscles and reduce your breathing rate. Remember if you are having difficulty with continuous jumping or with

executing the footwork, go back to the neutral move by placing both handles in one hand and rotate the rope at the side of your body. The goal of jumping rope is to condition your cardiovascular system, so you want to keep your heart rate elevated. Try to work at a perceived exertion of 7 to 9.

▼ Jump Rope

Heavy Bag
(3 x 3-minute rounds)
Hit the bag for three-minutes, and then take a one-minute rest. Repeat three times. Starting in the classic boxing stance with your hands up, throw left jabs as you move around the bag. Your left jab is your range finder, so start by throwing plenty of jabs to establish an effective distance from the bag and set a good punching pace. Keep busy, ensuring your movement and combinations flow easily and there are no long pauses between punches. Start throwing 'one-two's' (a left jab followed by a straight right). Visualize an opponent in front of you and keep moving. Simulate a body attack by bending the legs and lowering your body hitting the mid-section of the bag. Find your rhythm and move naturally with the swinging motion of the bag. Find a consistent punching pace that you can continue with and persevere to the end of the round. For the second and third rounds, work on three and four punch combinations *(refer to Chapter 4)*. Keep moving during your one-minute rest, walking around the bag reducing the heart rate slightly and planning your next round. Work at a perceived exertion of 7 to 9.

▼ Heavy Bag

Punch Mitts
(2 x 3-minute rounds)
Partner Drill: When training on the punch mitts, concentrate on the proper execution of your punches and balanced footwork. Alternate the three-minute rounds with your partner, taking turns punching and catching. You will also be getting a workout even when you catch the punches. Keep the combinations basic, starting with the straight punches. Establish a pattern of throwing many crisp jabs, continually moving in between the throws. The catcher controls the action and sets the workout pace, calling out the combinations and keeping the puncher in view at all times. The puncher must remember to listen for the commands from the catcher, execute the punch and then move away, ready for the next command. As you become more comfortable throwing and catching punches, increase the speed and work on more complicated combinations *(refer to Chapter 5).*

No Partner Option: If you do not have partner, you can use the heavy bag as an alternate workout option.

▼ Punch Mitts

▼ Core Strength Training

Heavy Bag Ladder Drill
This drill challenges your straight punching technique, foot movement, upper body conditioning and endurance. Try to complete this drill within six minutes.

Ladder One: Throw twelve left jabs. Reduce the number of jabs you throw by one each time, continuing down the ladder until you throw just one jab.

Take a one minute rest.

Ladder Two: Throw twelve one-two punch combinations, (left jab-straight right). Reduce the number by one each time continuing down the ladder until you throw just one, one-two punch combination *(refer to Chapter 4).*

Shadowboxing Cool Down
(1 x 3-minute round)
Throw a variety of punches at fifty to sixty per cent effort. Even though you are not throwing as hard as you did during your workout it is still important to focus on the proper execution of the punches. Keep your feet moving side-to-side and front and back. Allow your heart rate to lower, catch your breath, and work at a perceived exertion of 3 to 4.

Core Strength Training
Select two to three medicine ball exercises to work your core muscles *(refer to Chapter 7).*

Sample Sequence:

Medicine Ball Crunch
10 to 20 repetitions with a 3 to 5 kg (6 to 12 lb) medicine ball.
Perform two to three sets.

Overhead Pull-Up
10 to 15 repetitions with a 3 to 5 kg (6 to 10 lb) medicine ball.
Perform two to three sets.

Seated Bent Knee Tuck
10 to 15 repetitions with a 3 to 5 kg (6 to 10 lb) medicine ball.
Perform two to three sets.

Side Pullover Sit-Up
10 to 15 repetitions with a 3 to 5 kg (6 to 10 lb) medicine ball.
Perform two to three sets.

Stretch
Select specific stretches for all the main muscle groups you have trained. Hold each stretch for 30 to 60 seconds *(refer to Chapter 8).*

THE BASIC WORKOUT SUMMARY
3-Day/Week Program

Shadowboxing Warm-Up
(1 x 3-minute round)
Shadowbox working on the basic punches. Focus on proper technique.

Shadowboxing *(1 x 3-minute round)*
Add more movement while throwing more punches and combinations. Add more intent to the punches. *(Refer to Chapter 2)*

Jump Rope *(3 x 3-minute rounds)*
Jump for three-minutes straight, take a one-minute break and repeat jumping for two more rounds with a one-minute break in between. *(Refer to Chapter 3)*

Heavy Bag
(3 x 3-minute rounds)
Hit the bag for three minutes, and then take a one-minute rest. Repeat three times. Ensure your foot movement is balanced and your punch combinations flow. *(Refer to Chapter 4)*

Punch Mitts *(2 x 3-minute rounds)*

Partner Drill: Alternate with your partner taking turns punching and catching. *(Refer to Chapter 5)*

No Partner Option:
Heavy Bag Ladder Drill (6 minutes)
Ladder One: Throw twelve left jabs, reducing down to one jab. Take a one-minute rest.
Ladder Two: Throw twelve one-two punch combinations, reducing down to one-two punch combination. *(Refer to Chapter 4)*

Shadowboxing to Cool Down
(1 x 3-minute round)
End with shadowboxing, punching with light intent. Reduce your heart rate.

Strength Training
Sample Sequence:
Medicine Ball Crunch, Overhead Pull-Up, Seated Bent Knee Tuck, Side Pullover Sit-Up. *(Refer to Chapter 7)*

Stretch
Allow time to properly stretch out all the muscle groups and joint areas. *(Refer to Chapter 8)*

THE CONTENDER WORKOUT PROGRAM

5 Day/Week Program
10 Weeks

The Contender workout bumps up the intensity to a five-day program for 10 weeks and requires a more serious commitment. The boxing training workout is performed three days a week and includes working on the heavy bag, jumping rope, shadowboxing, focus mitt training, double-end bag training,

and speed-bag work. In between your boxing training days are 'Active Rest Days'. On these days, roadwork and strength training with the medicine ball are performed. The roadwork and strength training will compliment your boxing conditioning. Make a commitment to follow the Contender workout for 10 weeks.

BOXING WORKOUT DAYS...
Day 1, 3, 5

For example: Monday, Wednesday, and Friday

Shadowboxing Warm-up
(1 x 3-minute round)
Move around to warm up your muscles and throw easy punches to start. Focus on the execution of your punches, beginning with straight punches and then adding hooks and uppercuts. Continue moving for three minutes.

▼ Shadowboxing

Rest for one minute, walking around and stretching out any muscles that feel tight. Loosen up the shoulders, hip flexors and legs *(refer to Chapter 8)*.

Shadowboxing
(2 x 3-minute rounds)
Remember, shadowboxing is like being in the ring with an opponent. Visualize your opponent in front of you, move and punch, making use of the available floor space. Now that you have warmed up put more power behind your punches. Have a plan. Stay light on your feet and execute your punch combinations with balanced footwork. Practice mixing slips and ducks into your combinations, developing offensive and defensive moves. For the last round you may want to hold onto light hand weights (1 to 2 kg, .5 to 1 lb) punching at 60 per cent intensity. For more information on shadowboxing refer to Chapter 2. Work at a perceived exertion of 6 to 7.

Rest for one-minute in between the shadowboxing rounds. Remember to allow your heart rate to come down slightly, keep moving around, and stretch out tight muscles.

Jump Rope
(9 to 12 minute continuous jumping)
Jump rope continuously for 9 to 12 minutes, mixing up the jumps and the intensity. For the first two minutes jump at a moderate pace, gradually increasing the speed and mixing up the footwork. Perform footwork patterns like

▼ Jump Rope

the Ali shuffle, scissors, and front crosses. Travel forward and backward and side-to-side, staying light on your feet *(refer to Chapter 3)*. Work at a perceived exertion of 7 to 9.

Jump Rope Ladder Option
Another option is to perform the jump rope ladder drill in place of jumping continuously. Choose a number of jumps to start. For example: 400 - count 400 jumps. Take a 30 to 60-second rest and then reduce the number of jumps by 50 for each ladder, 350 jumps, rest, 300 jumps, rest, 250, rest and so forth *(refer to Chapter 3)*.

Punch Mitts
(3 x 3-minute rounds)
If you are training with a partner alternate the 3 x 3-minute rounds with your partner, taking turns punching and catching. The puncher needs to focus on throwing fast accurate punches at the mitts, developing a smooth rhythm, and staying balanced. Catchers need to challenge their partner and set the pace. Remember working together as a team is the key when training on punch mitts. Incorporate a multitude of punch combinations that include slipping and ducking *(refer to Chapter 5)*.

Ladder Punch Drill
Finish off your punch mitt training with the Ladder Punch Drill by throwing the one-two punch combination at the punch mitts and then dropping and performing push-ups. Start with eight 1-2's and eight push-ups for a total 36 punches/36 push-ups, working down to one of each *(refer to Chapter 5)*.

If you do not have a partner to catch for you, go directly to the bag workouts.

Heavy Bag
(4 x 3-minute rounds)
At the Contender level you should be performing a greater variety of punches and punch combinations with fluid footwork and balanced body movement. Visualize an opponent in front

▼ Heavy Bag

of you as you punch. Add slips and feints staying light on your feet. Mix up your punches by throwing to the body area and head area of the bag. Always keep your hands up in the on-guard position as you move around the bag. Sustain a good punching pace for the entire three-minutes of every round and use your one-minute rest to recover between rounds. Keep moving during the one-minute rest period and focus on the next round. Work at a perceived exertion of 7 to 9.

Complete three more heavy bag rounds and finish off working on the bag by performing 'heavy bag sprints'. Refer to Chapter 4 if you want to substitute with a different drill.

Heavy Bag Drill
Speed Sprints
Face the heavy bag straight on with both arms at an equal distance from the bag for the entire drill. Hit the bag continuously as fast as you can with a one-two, one-two rhythm. Keep your core held tight, weight centred through the balls of the feet, knees relaxed, and a steady breathing rate. Sprint for 25 seconds, rest for 25 seconds and repeat two more times. In the following weeks,

increase your sprint time to 30 seconds, then 35 seconds, with the equivalent rest times. Always keep moving and walking around during the rest intervals. For your last sprint, work at a perceived exertion of 9 to 10. Take a two-minute rest before working on the double-end bag.

▼ Speed Bag

Double-End Bag
(1 x 3-minute round)
If a double-end bag is available work on it for one round, perfecting the timing and speed of your punches, and the side-to-side movement of your head and body *(refer to Chapter 4)*. Rest for one-minute before hitting the speed bag.

Speed Bag
(2 x 3-minute rounds)
Working out on the speed bag helps to develop hand-eye coordination and challenges your upper body endurance. Concentrate on striking the bag correctly to keep it moving smoothly *(refer to Chapter 4)*. Rest for one-minute between rounds.

Shadowboxing Cool Down
(1 x 3-minute round)
Throw light punches working on technique and allow your heart rate to lower. Reduce your breathing rate and work at a perceived exertion of 3 to 4.

▼ Shadowboxing Cool Down

Core Strength Training

Select two to three medicine ball exercises to work your core muscles *(refer to Chapter 7)*.

Sample Sequence:

Medicine Ball Crunch
100 repetitions with a 3 to 5 kg (6 to 12 lb) medicine ball. If you prefer, break up the repetitions into two sets of 50, with a 30-second break in between.

Medicine Ball Ab-Press
15 repetitions with a 3 to 5 kg (6 to 10 lb) medicine ball. Perform two to three sets.

V-Ups
10-15 repetitions with a 3 to 4 kg (6 to 8 lb) medicine ball. Perform two to three sets.

Stretch

Perform stretching exercises holding each stretch for 30 to 60 seconds, *(refer to Chapter 8)*.

ROADWORK AND STRENGTH TRAINING... Days 2, 4

For example: Tuesday and Thursday

On your non-boxing training days, perform either roadwork or strength training. If you choose both, perform your roadwork first, followed by strength training.

Roadwork

Depending on your fitness level and running ability, select one of the running programs from Chapter 6, Run like a Boxer. Several options are provided such as Just Starting Out, Staying in Shape, Crank It Up, Intervals Sprints and Hill Runs.

▼ Core Strength Training

▼ Roadwork

▼ Strength Training

Strength Training

Select the basic, intermediate, or advanced medicine ball workouts from Chapter 7 or you can perform the following sequences.

Sample Sequences:

Full Body
Woodchopper
10 to 12 repetitions, holding a 3 to 4 kg (6 to 8 lb) medicine ball. Perform two to three sets.

Medicine Ball Burpees
12 to 15 repetitions. Select a medicine ball that is larger in size to give you a more stable base. Perform two to three sets.

Upper Body
Staggered Push-Ups
10 to 12 repetitions. Select a medicine ball that is larger in size to give you a more stable base. Perform two sets.

Core
Side Pullover Sit-Up
10 to 15 repetitions with a 3 to 5 kg (6 to 10 lb) medicine ball. Perform one to two sets.

▼ Stretch

V-Ups
10 to 15 repetitions with a 3 to 4 kg (6 to 8 lb) medicine ball. Perform two to three sets.

Medicine Ball Ab-Press
15 repetitions, holding a 3 to 5 kg (6 to 10 lb) medicine ball. Perform three sets.

Medicine Ball Plank
Hold for 30 seconds, increasing to 60 seconds. Perform two to three sets.

Lower Body
Power Squats
10 to 15 repetitions holding a 3 to 5 kg (6 to12 lb) medicine ball. Perform one to two sets.

Forward Lunges
10 to 20 repetitions for each leg holding a 4 to 7 kg (8 to 15 lb) medicine ball. Perform two to three sets.

Stretch
Select stretches for all the main muscle groups you have trained. Hold each stretch for 30 to 60 seconds *(refer to Chapter 8)*.

THE CONTENDER WORKOUT PROGRAM SUMMARY
5-Day/Week Program – for 10 Weeks

Shadowboxing Warm-Up
(1 x 3 minute round)
Warm up your muscles and throw easy punches to start.

Shadowboxing *(2 x 3 minute rounds)*
Increase the intensity of your punches. *(Refer to Chapter 2).*

Jump Rope *(9 to 12 minutes)*
Jump rope continuously for 9 to 12 minutes, mixing up your footwork. *(Refer to Chapter 3)*

Punch Mitts *(3 x 3-minute rounds)*
Alternate catching and punching rounds with your partner. Include a multitude of punch combinations that include slipping and ducking. *(Refer to Chapter 5)*

Punch Mitt Drill
Ladder Punch Drill
Perform eight 1-2's and eight push-ups for a total of 36 punches/36 push-ups, working down to one of each *(refer to Chapter 5)*. If you do not have a partner go directly to the bag workouts.

Heavy Bag
(4 x 3-minute rounds)
Challenge yourself by throwing a wide variety of punch combinations. Sustain a good punching pace for the entire three-minutes of every round. *(Refer to Chapter 4)*

Heavy Bag Drill
Speed Sprints
Sprint for 25 seconds, rest for 25 seconds and repeat two more times. Increase your sprint time to 30 seconds, then 35 seconds, with the equivalent rest time.

Sprint 1   25 seconds (rest 25 seconds)
Sprint 2   25 seconds (rest 25 seconds)
Sprint 3   25 seconds (rest 25 seconds)

Double-End Bag
(1 x 3 minute round)
Work one round on the double-end bag, perfecting the timing and speed of your punches and the side-to-side movement of your head and body. *(Refer to Chapter 4)*

Speed Bag
(2 x 3 minute rounds)
Work out on the speed bag maintaining a smooth rhythm and fast pace. *(Refer to Chapter 4)*

Shadowboxing Cool Down
(1 x 3 minute round)
Throw light punches working on technique. Allow your heart rate to lower.

Strength Training
(4 to 6 minutes)
Medicine Ball Crunch, Medicine Ball Ab-Press, V-Ups. *(Refer to Chapter 7)*

Stretch
Allow time to properly stretch out all the muscle groups and joint areas. *(Refer to Chapter 8)*

ROADWORK AND STRENGTH TRAINING

Roadwork *(30 to 45 minutes)*
Select a roadwork program appropriate to your fitness level, from Chapter 6.

Strength Training
Select a medicine ball strength training routine form Chapter 7 or perform the exercises from the sample sequence. Woodchopper, Medicine Ball Burpee, Staggered Push-up, Side Pullover Sit-up, V-Ups, Medicine Ball Ab-Press, Medicine Ball Plank, Power Squats, Forward Lunges.

Stretch
Allow time to properly stretch out all the muscle groups and joint areas *(refer to Chapter 8)*.

THE CHAMP'S WORKOUT PROGRAM

6 Day/Week Program
12 Weeks

For the Champs workout, an extra day of training is added for a total of 6 days per week over a 12-week period. The training intensity level is increased, and a focused commitment is required. Perform the boxing workout 3 times per week, and on the alternate active rest days, perform roadwork and strength training with the medicine ball. Take advantage of the one day off to recover from the six days of training.

The boxing workout includes the heavy bag, jump rope, shadowboxing, punch mitts, double-end bag, speed bag, and strength training with the medicine ball. The active rest days include roadwork, sprints, and strength training with the medicine ball.

BOXING WORKOUT DAYS.... Day 1, 3, 5

Perform on alternate days. For example: Monday, Wednesday, and Friday.

Shadowboxing Warm-Up
(1 x 3-minute round)
Throw light punches to start, focusing on proper execution. Begin with straight punches and then add hooks and uppercuts. Continue moving for three-minutes.

Shadowboxing *(2 x 3-minute rounds)*
Now that you have warmed up, put more power and intensity behind your punches. Move and throw punches at your 'virtual opponent'. Practice offensive and defensive moves *(refer to Chapter 2)*.

▼ Shadowboxing Warm-Up

▼ The Champ's Workout

▼ Punch Mitts

Jump Rope
(Continuous for 15 to 20 minutes)
For your jump rope training session, start by jumping at a moderate pace for the first few minutes to set your jumping rhythm. Challenge yourself by adding a variety of footwork and rope moves. Perform double unders, cross-overs, and speed sprints within your training. Finish off with a two to three-minute cool down, reducing the pace of your jumps *(refer to Chapter 3)*.

Punch Mitts
(4 x 3-minute rounds)
Punch mitt training allows you to bring all of your fitness boxing skills into play. This dynamic training sharpens your punching skills, defensive moves, reflexes, balance, and develops upper body strength and endurance. At the Champs level you want to throw a wide variety of punch combinations and at a

higher level of intensity. If you are proficient at executing the advanced combinations described in Chapter 5, you may want to develop your own punch combinations. When creating your own combinations ensure a logical sequence is followed and that each punch smoothly sets up the next punch or movement.

Punch Mitt Drill

Punch Mitt Sprints
This rapid-fire series of straight punches, hooks, uppercuts, slipping, and ducking challenges and develops your cardio endurance. Maintain a quick pace and execute the punches with proper technique. Begin with 20-second sprints and increase the time increment to 30 to 40-second sprints. Repeat the sprint sequence twice and then switch roles with your training partner *(refer to Chapter 5)*.

Sprint One

Straight lefts and rights	20 seconds
Left and right hooks	20 seconds
Left and right uppercuts	20 seconds
Slipping side-to-side	20 seconds

Sprint Two

Straight lefts and rights	20 seconds
Left and right hooks	20 seconds
Left and right uppercuts	20 seconds
Ducking under	20 seconds

It is important to modify punch mitt workouts to each individual's ability and skill level. This is accomplished by adapting the intensity level and the punch sequencing of the drill.

Heavy Bag

(5 x 3-minute rounds)
Train on the heavy bag as though you are facing an actual opponent in the ring, constantly moving while throwing punch combinations. Include feints, slips, and ducking moves into the mix and visualize deceiving your opponent in order to set up punching opportunities *(refer to Chapter 4)*. Adding these subtle movements adds another

▼ Heavy Bag

element to your heavy bag training. Coordinate your footwork and punches with the swinging motion of the bag. Remember real boxing matches do not have long periods of inactivity. Throw plenty of punches and keep moving to simulate real fight situations. Move around during the one-minute rest period and plan your next round. Work at a perceived exertion of 7 to 9.

Theme Your Rounds

When hitting the heavy bag, theme your rounds by emulating different boxing styles. For example, for one round simulate the style of boxers who have incredible footwork and hand speed, such as Muhammad Ali and Sugar Ray Leonard. The challenge is to constantly move and change direction while firing off long range punches. In your next round emulate the style of a close-range, inside fighter. Champion Gennady Golovkin continually moves forward to land powerful hooks and uppercuts. Working on different fighting styles allows you to get the maximum out of your Ultimate Boxing Workout.

Heavy Bag Drill

(1 x 3-minute round)
30/30/30
Move around the bag and execute a series of fast punches for 30 seconds. Now face the bag straight on, punching and running on the spot lifting your knees high. For the last 30 seconds return to the boxing stance and go all out like you are trying to knock out your opponent. Complete the sequence twice without stopping to complete the three-minute round *(refer to Chapter 4)*. Working at a perceived exertion of 8 to 9. Take a one-to-two minute rest before hitting the double-end bag.

Double-End Bag

(2 x 3-minute rounds)
Throw punch combinations and slips ensuring you are in a balanced position reacting to the quick movement and the rebound action of the double-end bag. Develop your timing and rhythm

▼ Double-End Bag

constantly moving and firing rapid-fire punches *(refer to Chapter 4)*. Rest for one minute in between rounds and before hitting the speed bag.

Speed Bag
(6 to 8 minutes)
Challenge your upper body endurance by hitting the speed bag at a fast pace for six to eight minutes. Rest for one-minute before moving onto the shadowboxing.
NOTE: If you do not have a double-end bag or speed bag, shadowbox for two additional rounds.

Shadowboxing Cool Down
(1 x 3-minute round)
Focus on proper technique as you move and throw punches during this final cool-down round. Gradually slow down your movements and reduce your breathing rate. By the end of the cool down round you should be at a perceived exertion of 3 to 4.

Core Strength – Medicine Ball
Select two medicine ball strength exercises to train your core region *(refer to Chapter 7)*.

Sample Sequence:

Medicine Ball Cycle
30 to 40 repetitions, holding a 3 to 5 kg (6 to 10 lb) medicine ball. Perform two sets.

Roll-Up and Knee Tuck
10 to 15 repetitions with a 3 to 4 kg (6 to 8 lb) medicine ball. Perform two to three sets.

Core Strength – Punch Mitts
(2-minutes)
Punch Mitt Abdominal Punch-Up Drill: complete two sets of 30-second straight punches, hooks and uppercuts *(refer to Chapter 4)*.

If you have a partner perform punch mitts abs. If not, select another core exercise from Chapter 7.

▼ Stretch

Stretch
Perform stretching exercises holding each stretch for 30 to 60 seconds *(refer to Chapter 8)*.

ROADWORK AND STRENGTH TRAINING

Perform on alternate days.
For example: Tuesday, Thursday, and Saturday.

Roadwork
Perform your roadwork training first. Include intervals, sprints, and an occasional aerobic longer run *(refer to Chapter 6)*.

Intervals
Jog for one Km at a moderate pace to warm-up. Pick up the pace and run for 200 or 400 metres, (or one-minute to two-minutes) at a perceived exertion of 6 to 7. Now bump up the intensity for the next interval and run a distance of 200 or 400, (or one-minute to two-minutes) at a perceived exertion to 8 to 9. Repeat the intervals six times. Finish off with an easy one to two Km jog.

Distance Sprints
One day a week, include sprint work during the interval sessions.
Sample Routine:
Warm up by jogging for 400 metres. Sprint for 200 metres, six times at a perceived exertion level of 9 to 10. Keep

▼ Core Strength – Medicine Ball

up this running intensity for the entire distance and then jog or walk back (200 metres) to your starting point. Repeat six times. Jog for 800 metres to cool down after your last interval.

Strength Training

Select eight to twelve medicine ball exercises to work your full body, upper body, core, and lower body *(refer to Chapter 7)*.

Sample Sequences:

Full Body
Rock 'n' Roll
10 to 12 repetitions, holding a 3 to 4 kg (6 to 8 lb) medicine ball. Perform two to three sets.

Mountain Climber
12 to 15 repetitions or for 20 to 40 seconds using a larger sized medicine ball. Perform two to three sets.

Upper Body
The Boxer's Push-Up
8 to 12 repetitions using a larger sized medicine ball. Perform two to three sets.

Standing Medicine Ball Twist
8 to 12 repetitions with a 3 to 5 kg (6 to 10 lb) medicine ball. Perform one to three sets.

▼ Strength Training

Core
Overhead Pull-Ups
10 to 15 repetitions with a 3 to 5 kg (6 to 10 lb) medicine ball. Perform two to three sets.

Medicine Ball Ab-Press
15 repetitions, holding a 3 to 5 kg (6 to 10 lb) medicine ball. Perform two to three sets.

Side Pullover Sit-Up
10 to 15 repetitions with a 3 to 5 kg (6 to 10 lb) medicine ball. Perform two sets.

Roll-Up and Knee Tuck
10 to 15 repetitions with a 3 to 4 kg (6 to 8 lb) medicine ball. Perform two to three sets.

Seated Bent Knee Tuck
10 to 15 repetitions with a 3 to 5 kg (6 to 10 lb) medicine ball. Perform one to three sets.

Lower Body
180's
12 to 15 repetitions or for 20-40 seconds, using a 3 to 4 kg (6 to 8 lb) medicine ball. Perform one to two sets.

THE CHAMP'S WORKOUT PROGRAM SUMMARY
6-Day/Week Program – for 12 Weeks

Shadowboxing Warm-Up
(1 x 3-minute round)
Gradually warm-up and prepare for your workout.

Shadowboxing *(2 x 3-minute rounds)*
Pick up the pace. Move and throw punches at your 'virtual opponent'. *(Refer to Chapter 2)*

Jump Rope
(Continuous for 15-20 minutes)
Challenge yourself by adding a variety of footwork and rope moves. Finish off with a two to three-minute cool down. *(Refer to Chapter 3)*

Punch Mitts *(4 x 3-minute rounds)*
Throw a wide a variety of punch combinations, at a high level of intensity. *(Refer to Chapter 5)*

Punch Mitt Sprints

Sprint One
Straight lefts and rights	30 seconds
Left and right hooks	30 seconds
Left and right uppercuts	30 seconds
Slipping side-to-side	30 seconds

Sprint Two
Straight lefts and rights	30 seconds
Left and right hooks	30 seconds
Left and right uppercuts	30 seconds
Ducking under	30 seconds

Heavy Bag *(5 x 3-minutes rounds)*
Constantly move while throwing punch combinations including feints, slips, and ducks into the mix. *(Refer to Chapter 4)*

Heavy Bag Drill *(1 x 3-minute round)*
Dirty 30s
Box for 30 seconds, high knees and punch for 30 seconds, and power punch for 30 seconds. Repeat the sequence to complete the three-minute round. *(Refer to Chapter 4)*.

Double-End Bag *(2 x 3-minute rounds)*
Throw punch combination and slips. *(Refer to Chapter 4)*.

Speed Bag *(6 – 8 minutes)*
Strike the speed bag at a fast pace for six to eight minutes.

Shadowboxing Cool Down
(1 x 3-minute round)
Throw your punches lightly to cool down.

Core Strength - Medicine Ball
Medicine Ball Cycle and Roll-Up and Knee Tuck.

Core Strength – Punch Mitts
Punch Mitt Abdominal Punch-Up Drill *(refer to Chapter 5)*. If you have a partner perform focus mitts abs. If not select another core exercise from Chapter 7.

Stretch
Allow time to properly stretch out all the muscle groups and joint areas. *(Refer to Chapter 8)*

Forward Lunges
10 to 20 repetitions for each leg holding a 4 to 7 kg (8 to 15 lb) medicine ball. Perform two to three sets.

Power Squats
10 to 15 repetitions holding a 3 to 5 kg (6 to 12 lb) medicine ball. Perform one to two sets.

Stretch
Select stretches for all the main muscle groups you have trained. Hold each stretch for 30 to 60 seconds *(refer to Chapter 8)*.

ROADWORK AND STRENGTH TRAINING

Roadwork
Jog at an easy pace for one Km to warm-up. Perform interval work (distance 200 to 400 metres or timed at one-two minutes) Include timed sprints, distance sprints or hill sprints. Finish with an easy run *(refer to Chapter 6)*.

Strength Training
Perform 10 to 12 exercises (Chapter 7). Rock 'n' Roll, Mountain Climber, Upper Body, The Boxer's Push-Up, Standing Medicine Ball Twist, Overhead Pull-Ups, Medicine Ball Ab-Press, Side Pullover Sit-Up, Roll-Up and Knee Tuck, Seated Bent Knee Tuck, 180's, Forward Lunges, Power Squats

Stretch
Allow time to properly stretch out all the muscle groups and joint areas *(refer to Chapter 8)*.

12-ROUND CHALLENGE SUMMARY

Round 1 - Shadowboxing Warm-Up
(1 x 3-minute round)
Gradually warm-up and prepare for your workout.

Round 2, 3, 4, 5 - Heavy Bag
(4 x 3-minutes rounds)
Perform various combinations.
(Refer to Chapter 4)

Round 6 - Heavy Bag Drill
(1 x 3-minute round)
Dirty 30s
Box for 30 seconds, high knees and punch for 30 seconds, and power punch for 30 seconds. Repeat the sequence to complete the three-minute round.
(Refer to Chapter 4)

Round 7, 8, 9 - Punch Mitts
(3 x 3-minute rounds)
Throw a wide a variety of punch combinations, at a high level of intensity.
(Refer to Chapter 5)

Round 10 - Double-End Bag
(1 x 3-minute round)
Throw punch combination and slips.
(Refer to Chapter 4)

Round 11 – Speed Bag
(1 x 3-minute round)
Strike the speed bag at a fast pace for three minutes. *(Chapter 4)*

Round 12 – Shadowboxing Cool Down
(1 x 3-minute round)
Throw your punches lightly to cool down.

12-ROUND CHALLENGE

Three-minute rounds, 1-minute rest
Total time: 49 minutes

This is a no jump-rope workout routine. The drills focus on punching power, execution, and speed.

Warm-up by shadowboxing at a good pace for three-minutes. With your hands wrapped and your gloves on, complete four rounds on the heavy bag. Include various combinations, visualizing an opponent, moving around, and throwing lots of punches.

Next perform the heavy bag drill, Dirty 30s. This drill varies the punching pace every 30 seconds in a three-minute round. For the next three rounds (7, 8, 9) select combinations from the Punch Mitt Chapter Five training with your partner. Work on your agility and timing with one round on the double-end bag and one round on the speed bag. Finally, cool-down for three minutes, reducing your heart and breathing rate.

15-ROUND KNOCKOUT

Three-minute rounds, 1-minute rest
Total Time – 59 minutes

The 15-Round Knockout routine provides an authentic old school boxing training experience.

Shadowbox for three-minutes to warm-up. Grab your rope and perform a variety of jumps for four rounds, taking a one-minute rest in between the rounds. Wrap your hands and put on your gloves to perform four rounds on the heavy bag. With a partner work on Punch Mitt drills for the next three rounds. Then, work on your agility and timing with one round on the double-end bag and one round on the speed bag. Perform a cool-down round by shadowboxing for three minutes.

15-ROUND
KNOCKOUT SUMMARY

Round 1 - Shadowboxing Warm-Up
(1 x 3-minute round)
Gradually warm-up and prepare for your workout.

Round 2, 3, 4, 5 – Jump Rope
(4 x 3-minute rounds)
Perform a variety of footwork and rope moves. *(Refer to Chapter 3)*

Round 6, 7, 8, 9 – Heavy Bag
(4 x 3-minutes rounds)
Perform various combinations.
(Refer to Chapter 4)

Round 10, 11, 12 – Punch Mitts
(3 x 3-minute rounds)
Throw a wide a variety of punch combinations, at a high level of intensity.
(Refer to Chapter 5)

Round 13- Double-End Bag
(1 x 3-minute round)
Throw punch combination and slips.
(Refer to Chapter 4)

Round 14 – Speed Bag
(1 x 3-minute round)
Strike the speed bag at a fast pace for three minutes. *(Chapter 4)*

Round 15 – Shadowboxing Cool Down
(1 x 3-minute round)
Throw your punches lightly to cool down.

BOXING FOR FITNESS AT A PRIVATE CLUB

More and more gyms are offering boxing-style classes, as well as private instruction with a trainer. Many boxing clubs are now offering workout programs, some including sparring.

If you are searching for a boxing-style fitness class look for a facility that has boxing equipment, such as heavy bags, double-end bags, and speed bags. Ensure there is sufficient space to jump rope, work on punch mitts with a partner, and mirrors to check your punch execution and movement. Work with trainers who are certified with a recognized boxing/fitness association. Take time to watch a training session before you make your decision to participate. A trainer should be knowledgeable and approachable, and give clear, positive, and direct instruction and feedback. A good trainer will bring out the best in you and provide a fun, safe, and effective workout that meets all of your fitness goals.

A GOOD TRAINER WILL BRING OUT THE BEST IN YOU AND PROVIDE A FUN, SAFE, AND EFFECTIVE WORKOUT THAT MEETS ALL OF YOUR FITNESS GOALS.

▼ Round Knockout Workout

THE GREAT BOXING CHAMPIONS AND TRAINERS, PAST AND PRESENT, HAVE INSPIRED THE DEVELOPMENT OF THE ULTIMATE BOXING WORKOUT. GREAT BOXERS SHOW A PASSION AND A DEDICATION TO PERFECTING THEIR CRAFT AND TO ACHIEVING SUPERB PHYSICAL CONDITIONING. THEY KNOW EVERYTHING MEANINGFUL IN LIFE RESULTS FROM HARD WORK AND PUTTING IN AN HONEST EFFORT.

▼ Andy with Muhammad Ali

▼ Jamie with Roy Jones Jr.

The Ultimate Boxing Workouts stay true to the origins and the spirit of boxing. It provides exhilarating and authentic boxing workouts for improved overall fitness. Success comes from doing little things correctly, day in and day out. Continue to practice and improve, working the fundamentals and strive to get better each and everyday. We hope the information provided in this book will provide you with years of fun, challenging, and effective workouts.

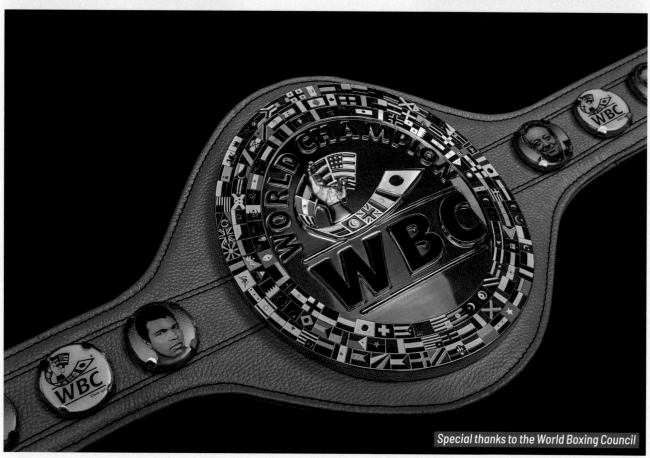

Special thanks to the World Boxing Council

www.ultimateboxingworkout.com

CHAPTER FOUR   *Punching Bag Workouts*

CHAPTER FIVE   *Punch Mitt Workouts*

ULTIMATE BOXING WORKOUT